BEYOND the code

BEYOND the code

Setting You up for Success
as a Software Engineer

Dr. Christoph Kerschbaumer

BEYOND the code
Setting You up for Success
as a Software Engineer

Design   Sabine Kerschbaumer
                    https://sabinekerschbaumer.com
Editorial   Peter Saint-Andre
                    https://stpeter.im
Photography   Werner Kmetitsch
                    https://wernerkmetitsch.com

To all software engineers who want to rise above and grow beyond their code.

// Contents

BEYOND the code

Compiling
a New
Mental Program

*»Success comes to those who become
success conscious.« – Napoleon Hill*

Over the past two decades I've had the pleasure of collaborating with a diverse range of highly skilled software engineers. All fabulous human beings with outstanding technical capabilities and certainly some of the brightest minds on our planet.

Throughout these 20 years I've experienced first-hand the distinct operating principles of different engineers. More importantly, I've observed what the most successful engineers do to accelerate their growth and to maximize their impact.

As a Silicon Valley engineering manager, I have amassed beneficial insights by being in thousands of one-on-one meetings with some of the leading software engineers in the world. They willingly let me in on their secrets and shared valuable insights regarding the practices they used to expedite their career development. It is impressive to learn what habits they employ on a daily basis to unlock their full potential.

Moreover I was able to verify the effectiveness of their techniques throughout countless status update meetings as well as during international conferences, conventions, summits and all sorts of team and company-wide sessions.

This book summarizes my findings regarding what it takes to become truly successful as a software engineer. As a result, you too can benefit from these observations and insights.

I assure you, applying the suggestions outlined in the following chapters will boost your career over the long haul. It doesn't matter if you are an entry-level developer or a senior engineer. It doesn't matter if you are still in high school, in college, or pursuing a PhD in any of the software related fields. In fact, the habits outlined in this book are equally important and applicable at every level of software engineering.

< 6 >

Technical Skills Are Vital

There is absolutely no doubt that you need to master the domains of algorithms, data structures, and coding itself to become successful as a software engineer. Inarguably those core skills build the foundation for being a profound engineer in the first place. You cannot succeed as a software engineer if you do not have the skillset to write sophisticated, secure, and performant code. Some code reviewers even argue that »your code needs to read like a poem« before it can be merged into the codebase. (That's the best code review comment I've ever encountered. I still have a good laugh whenever I think about it.)

As fun and exciting as it is to solve problems using software, solely focusing on heads-down engineering work isn't enough to turbocharge your success. Over the years, I realized that you can't invest your energy exclusively on writing code and exploring the far corners of your favorite programming languages. In a modern setting it is indispensable to apply a more holistic approach for advancing your career if you want to become truly successful. More concretely, you not only need to commit code but you also need to commit to yourself.

< 7 >

Don't make the mistake of thinking that creating massive amounts of great code is »the only thing« you need to do. Question your fundamental beliefs if you think that merely generating and contributing code puts you in the fast lane to success.

```
>_ not only
   commit code
   but also
   commit to yourself
```

Truly successful software engineers take a step back, see the bigger picture, and consider a more holistic approach. They apply habits that enable them to grow faster and to have an impact that is far bigger than any piece of code they can ever merge into the codebase. They pay close attention to a multitude of factors that contribute to success, growth, and impact in the software business.

In short, they go »beyond the code«.

< 8 >

Let me be perfectly clear: To be successful in the software industry you definitely need to have sound engineering skills. You most definitely need to know and understand the principles and methods necessary to develop and produce complex, maintainable software systems. Furthermore, it is crucial to keep improving your engineering capabilities and to continuously acquire more technical skills. You can't stand still and rest on your laurels. The engineering world is constantly changing and you need to keep up with all the advancements in the software field so you can stay on the cutting edge.

However, I have also witnessed some of the best coders in the world remain just that: coders.

By contrast, I've also known engineers who went beyond the code and thus expanded their influence and impact unbelievably fast. Those engineers who understand and follow the suggestions outlined in this book are the ones who will grow ten times faster than ordinary engineers. Those engineers who internalize the habits collected in this book are the ones who will have an impact that is far bigger than the code they contribute. And those engineers who practice the recommendations in this book are the ones who will reach their goals ten times faster than the rest.

< 9 >

The most successful developers write code to perform specific tasks for the problems they want to solve, but they know that if all they do is contribute code then they will hit a ceiling in their career that blocks further advancement. They realize that they will remain on a lower rung of the career ladder for a long time if they just focus on coding with headphones on their ears and blinkers on their eyes.

>_ become more than just a coder

In summary, having sound technical skills is vital and lays the cornerstone for your success, but technical skills alone do not put you in the fast lane. If you want to acceler-ate your career advancement, then you need to go »beyond the code«. That's exactly what this book will help you do.

< 10 >

Update Your Default Settings

It is actually quite simple: if you want to grow and reach your full potential as a software engineer, then I recommend you follow the tried-and-true suggestions in this book. My goal is to give you some new mental files, a new mental program that you can compile for yourself. This new mental program opens you up to a new way of thinking, new habits, and therefore new and better results.

Think about it this way: the way you think made you what you are today. If you keep thinking and doing what you've always been doing, then you will keep getting what you always got. If instead you open yourself up and enhance your mind by reading the following chapters, your engineering life will be transformed.

You will see that adapting the suggestions presented in this book will enable you to get where you actually deserve to be. You will view things through a different lens, eliminate any blurry vision, and see a clear path to reaching your full potential.

Together we will analyze and question your established value system and evaluate the hierarchical order of that pyramid of values. We will reconfigure your expectations and build up your mind, which will create a clear picture

< 11 >

of your options and what is possible for you. In essence, we will install an update to your operating settings so you can craft and sign a new contract with yourself regarding what you can achieve in your career.

To ignite that crucial mindset shift, we will start by finding out what you really want. The story in the introductory chapter »Determine your Destination« is designed to help you identify who you really are. As a result, you will shift your perception and ultimately shape and create a mindset that focuses on success with laser sharp precision.

>_ compile the source code to transform your engineering life

More often than not, engineers who come to my coaching sessions are confused about their career goals, or have only a vague vision of what is possible for them. Quite of-

< 12 >

ten their default settings rely on an incorrectly established value system that causes them to unknowingly sabotage their own success.

>_ align
your actions
with your
goals

We want to make sure your actions are aligned with your goals right from the beginning. We further want you to become aware of your thoughts and also to make sure you can take full advantage of your options.

After we have established what you really want we move on to the core of this book, the 12 principles which will set you up for success as a software engineer. The pragmatic suggestions in these 12 chapters are designed to maximize the impact on your growth development.

< 13 >

Here's a brief preview of the 12 key principles that will help you to reach what you set out to accomplish. In the following chapters, we'll go into much greater detail on these principles for accelerating your career advancement.

1. Write Down Your Goals: Knowing what you want and who you would like to become are crucial for becoming successful. Only once you have identified what it is you actually want, can it become a tangible goal. By writing down your goals, you can eliminate distractions and focus on what you really want. We will also explore the advantages of logging your progress to always stay on track toward your destination.

2. Make Every Minute Count: Here we'll dispel the myth that you don't have time to achieve your goals. Instead, you have a choice and you are the one to decide how you invest your time and energy. We'll »take a look under the rug« and evaluate if you subconsciously create tasks that keep you busy but don't help you move forward. Then we'll shift your mindset so that you can continually make progress on the things that actually make a difference in your life and career.

< 14 >

3. Cultivate Your Communication: The way you communicate has a massive impact on your career and success. Although many people think of communication as an »outbound« process of writing and speaking, we'll also take a close look at the importance of listening. Only if you master all three of these skills you will be able to influence people to join your cause and assist you on your journey to become truly successful.

4. Create Solutions: We will explore and evaluate what problems are worth fixing, because the problems you choose to solve define who you are and who you will become. We will also help you get comfortable with taking calculated risks, because you can't create solutions and reach your goals without taking the right kind of risks.

5. Own Your Mistakes: Making mistakes »and owning those mistakes« are both essential for becoming successful. Mistakes are not the opposite of success; rather, mistakes are a natural part of the process and build the foundation for success. We'll also learn to see mistakes from a different angle and use them to make better decisions in the future.

6. Seek a Mentor: Mentors are those who are already years ahead of you on the path to success. Working with a mentor is extraordinarily powerful because it enables you to accelerate both your professional development and your personal development. We will also explore the benefits of being a mentor, because doing so can uncover unforeseen learning opportunities and further strengthen your sense of purpose in your engineering life.

7. Nourish Your Environment: No matter how smart you are, you can't do it alone. Success is not a zero-sum game - in fact it is the complete opposite, because success compounds. We'll look at the importance of supporting your colleagues, peers, and friends. If you keep feeding and supporting the people around you, then they will support and help you, too.

8. Ask Better Questions: When you ask questions, you engage more in every conversation and you gain and even absorb information faster. We'll drill down further by understanding how to ask the right questions, both of others and of yourself. And we'll see that it doesn't matter whether you need more resources for a project or even want a raise: if you don't ask, the answer is always no!

< 16 >

9. Be Persistent: Don't wait for tomorrow, but rather put in the effort today. Don't start out too big, but rather focus on the things you can do every single day to improve. When you put in even just a little effort every day, over time you will achieve big results. Ultimately we will strengthen your willpower so that you never give up.

10. Don't Take Things Personally: Never take things personally, because it only leads to negative emotions and unnecessary stress. By not taking things personally, you can protect your emotional well-being and maintain a positive mindset. In fact, you are the one who decides how to react to situations. When you choose not to take things personally, you can focus on the things that actually matter and make a difference.

11. Make No Excuses: It's critically important to hold yourself accountable for your actions - and also your inactions. By casting a critical eye on common types of excuses, we will transform your mindset and empower you to take complete ownership of your decisions. After that you will stop looking for excuses, but rather be honest with yourself and take responsibility for your actions. This inevitably has massive effects on your career.

< 17 >

12. Commit To Yourself: Finally, we will explore the key difference to becoming more successful, namely that you must commit to becoming successful. You are the only one who can decide if you'll procrastinate or instead put in the work and commit to yourself. You alone are in the driver's seat and you have the ability to create the results and the success you want to achieve in your life.

As you read through the chapters, I suggest that you stop frequently to reflect on yourself. Apply my suggestions at every opportunity and use them to solve your daily problems. Check up on the progress you are making each week and revisit the suggestions outlined in this book at regular intervals. Ask yourself what habits you have applied this week, what has worked well, and where you can improve. I really encourage you to develop a deep and intrinsically motivated desire to employ the suggestions presented in this book. I assure you that you will start to see positive results immediately.

>_   start
      to believe in
      yourself

< 18 >

Finally, let me suggest the following strategy, which has proven successful time and time again with the people I coach. Make an entertaining game out of your learning and really work on yourself to become better every single day.

Begin to believe in yourself and start to practice a »can-do attitude«. I know for a fact that the truly successful have established a core belief deep within themselves that they can reach whatever they set out to do, and I suggest you do the same.

Using the previous paragraphs as a catalyst for initiating your growth process, let's get started. Enjoy reading and remember:

You can do it!

< 19 >

< 20 >

Determine
Your
Destination

*»The journey of a thousand miles begins
with a single step.« – Lao Tzu*

Let's start our journey by considering a familiar but powerful analogy. Imagine that it's your birthday and you've received the best present ever: a brand new airplane! It's a big, magnificent plane with a living room, a bedroom, and a separate kitchen. In fact, it's big enough that you can bring your family, friends, and even your household pets.

Most likely you are imagining a place right now that you've always wanted to go visit. A faraway place you have pictured to yourself time and time again. A place that you just can't wait to see and experience. Chances are you have been dreaming and fantasizing about that certain place for a long time. Can you feel and sense the excitement you'll feel when you finally arrive at your destination?

Do you have a specific place in mind? Great! Envisioning and picturing this special place shows that you have the ability to visualize and determine your destination. So, what would you do next? Most likely you wouldn't waste a minute and would let the captain know exactly where you want to go, right?

Oh, I forgot to mention, the captain is part of the package, too. This is a special captain, one you have not encountered on any commercial airplane. The captain is »YOUR« captain, available and ready whenever you want to fly someplace new.

Your captain never needs to rest and is standing by twenty-four hours a day, seven days a week. Whenever you want to fly, your captain is already waiting for you in the cockpit warming up the engines. You can take off anytime, day or night, summer, spring, winter or fall.
Wow!

< 22 >

Now, let's come back to our defined destination – you still have that place in mind, right? For the purpose of this book let's pick Silicon Valley, a world-famous hub for technology companies and home to some of the world's best software engineers. With your destination in mind you might say: »Captain, can you please take me to San Francisco?«

With that simple statement, you would communicate clearly where you want to go. It's not a vague description, but a clear and precise definition of the destination.

Now let me provoke a thought experiment and ask you a different question. Would you ever say something like the following to the captain of your new plane? »Captain, let's take off right now and then let's just float in the air till we have decided where to go. We'll simply cruise around in circles till we have determined our destination. If we happen to run out of fuel, then so be it, we crash, but that's totally fine with me.«

>_ clearly define
who you
want to become

< 23 >

It's fair to assume that no sane human being would ever want to run out of fuel and crash their brand new airplane.

Yet, quite often when software engineers come to my coaching sessions and I ask them where they want to take their career, they initially cannot provide a precise answer. Oftentimes I hear them say that they are not sure, that they will just wait and see what happens. They don't know what their destination is!

>_ you can become
   highly successful
   if you have a vision

But if you don't know where you want to take your career, then it is essentially the same as telling your inner captain to take off with the plane and then see what happens. It is like hoping that you'll figure out where you want to go while already flying at cruising altitude. What I have realized as an engineer and manager is that truly successful software engineers know where they want to go. That's one thing exceptional engineers have in common and that sets

< 24 >

them apart from all the others. They know that having a goal and a clear vision for their future is crucial for their success. They know that having a well-defined destination is like owning a mental map that enables them to navigate even when the going gets tough.

Once you have clarity, then every decision you make from this point forward will be aligned with your mission and bring you closer to your destination. You won't take one step in the right direction and then another step in the opposite direction. Your inner captain, or inner compass if you will, will make sure you get closer to your goal and will prevent you from getting lost on the way.

>_ align every
   single decision
   with your mission

Of course, the weather won't always be sunny through-out your journey, there might be rain and gusty winds. However, your inner captain can adjust to situations while in the air and will prevent you from straying off course.

< 25 >

Once you have logged in the coordinates of where you want to go, that inner captain will take the fastest route possible and navigate directly to your destination.

Please note: believing in yourself and trusting that you are on the right path does not mean you are completely certain about everything. Rather, it means that you are generally heading in the right direction. That you don't constantly change your mind every other day based on a new outside stimulus or what other people are doing.

Making adjustments on your way is natural and expected, but having a clear destination enables you to ignore all the distractions on your journey.

>_ making progress
   towards your goals
   not only brings
   success but also
   true happiness

< 26 >

Once you have clarity, you will feel energized, you will feel like you are in the captain's seat and you will start to have greater control over your journey. In fact, having a well-defined goal allows you to bear pretty much anything along the way. Perhaps most importantly, once you know where you want to go, you can enjoy the flight. Making progress every day towards a goal you have defined brings not just success but true happiness.

< 27 >

< 28 >

CHAPTER 1

Write Down
Your Goals

*»People with goals succeed because
they know where they're going.«* – *Earl Nightingale*

Every success, grand victory, and outstanding accomplishment starts out as a thought in someone's mind. Before we can accomplish anything of value, we inevitably have to imagine it first. In the tech field, for every website, smartphone app, and software product, someone created a clear mental picture and managed to visualize a future where that thing would exist.

Put bluntly, if you can't imagine what you want, if you can't create a clear mental picture of that something, then you'll never be able to build it.

When getting to know the clients I work with, I love to ask a simple question: »What are your goals?« More often than not the answer I get is »I don't have any goals.« When I follow up, it often becomes apparent that the person across the table or on the video screen not only doesn't know what they want to achieve, but they don't even believe in the possibility of their own success.

Both knowing your goals and believing in yourself are essential ingredients for becoming truly successful. While in a later chapter we will explore why it is important to believe in yourself, this chapter focuses more sharply on figuring out your goals and clearly defining them.

So to begin, the first and imperative exercise for becoming more successful is to allocate time for yourself and to awaken all the unicorns in the land of your dreams. Create a safe space where you can allow your thoughts to wander around and fantasize about all the things you want to achieve. It is crucial to take the time and let loose so you can imagine and visualize what is possible for you in your career.

< 30 >

>_ picture who you want to become

This fundamental exercise, this straightforward thought experiment, is the starting point to get a sense of who you want to become. As the ancient Chinese sage Lao Tzu said, the journey of a thousand miles begins with a single step. This exercise is that single first step because it enables you to create and shape your future by thinking about what it is you actually want, which then ultimately can become your overarching goal.

I have done this exercise with multiple clients in my live coaching sessions and what I can recommend is the following: go for a long walk or hike. If possible, go hiking in nature. If you live in a city, take a stroll through a big park. Whatever you decide to do, make sure you are able to find a space for yourself where you feel comfortable and can let your thoughts wander around. It's best if you do this exercise all by yourself. Switch off all your electronic devices so no one can interrupt your session.

< 31 >

Keep in mind, this exercise is all about »YOU«.

Figure out what is important to »YOU«.

Figure out what »YOU« want.

Not what someone else wants or expects from you. Not what is important to your parents, your friends, your neighbors, your co-workers, or even your manager. No one can decide what is best for you, except you. So be honest with yourself. And when I say honest, I mean brutally honest. This exercise is purely about you, your aspirations, your vision for yourself, your goals.

The Power of Writing Down Goals

Now that you have been fantasizing and dreaming about your goals, it's time to shift gears. The fundamental lesson is that a dream remains only a dream if you don't act on it.

The dreams you don't act on eventually fizzle out because sooner or later they are replaced by a different dream. Now you want something else and you define a different goal in your mind. But if you don't act on »THAT« dream either, then the cycle just keeps on repeating.

< 32 >

>_ write down your goals so they can become reality

Writing down your goal helps you break that cycle. It makes implicit information explicit and hence enables you to keep your dream alive long enough to make it real. Only if you write down your aspirations can you lay the foundation for your dream to become a tangible goal. And once you have clearly defined your goal, you can aim for it and act on it.

Here is an easy exercise you can try for yourself. Once you have defined your goal, write it down on a piece of paper. Then take a deep breath and read it out loud. If a sense of fear comes up within you, then you know you have started on the path to something great.

The reason is simple: we have to expand our circle of confidence if we want to reach worthy goals. Expanding our circle of confidence, leaving our comfort zone, scares

< 33 >

us and causes fear to come up. It's worth noting that it's totally normal to feel and experience fear when setting tangible goals.

Every successful software engineer, in fact every true winner, has experienced fear. The difference is that winners persevere and act despite the fear. Winners don't allow fear to get in their way and block their road to success. I always tell my clients that experiencing fear is normal. In fact, experiencing fear is even positive. The best way to deal with fear is to simply acknowledge it. You can say something like this to yourself: »Hey fear, thanks for joining me on this epic journey. Without you I would be all by myself.« You will realize that fear is just a feeling that does not have the power to stop you. Simply acknowledging fear will set your mind at ease, allowing you to break free and start to move forward in the right direction.

How to Set Tangible Goals

First things first: a goal without an end date remains a dream. And if it is not measurable, then how will you know when you've reached your goal? Well, I suppose you won't. You'll still be flying around in your airplane, but the

< 34 >

captain - »you« - won't know when you've landed. Hence, a goal needs to meet the following three criteria so it counts as a tangible goal.

It needs to be (a) precise in its definition, (b) measurable, and (c) bound by a date.

Here is a specific example of a tangible goal: »By August 17th, I will have completely written and edited my book Beyond the Code which will contain 12 chapters and empower every software engineer to become truly successful.«

Let's evaluate together if this goal meets all the criteria and counts as a tangible goal: It is (a) precise in its definition, because it states that the goal is to write a book. It is (b) measurable, because it states explicitly that the book needs to contain 12 chapters. And finally (c) it is bound by a date, namely August 17th. Only if all three criteria are met does a goal really count as a tangible goal.

Of course, it's not productive to set completely unrealistic goals. But if you aim high then you are more likely to make significant progress. Here's an example. If I give you 300 days to develop an application, would you jump on it right away? Most likely not, because 300 days is a

< 35 >

long time from now. What if I give you only 30 days to do it? You would feel some form of urge and you would start working on it instantly.

Successful engineers expect a great deal of themselves and maintain a strong inner dialogue in which they hold themselves accountable for their success. They aim high and even if they slightly miss their target, they know how to adjust their goals, because they made it measurable in the first place.

When you make your goal measurable, specific, and bound by a date, then your brain starts operating in over-drive mode to achieve that goal. Otherwise it is too easy to fall back into hibernation mode and you are more likely to procrastinate.

>_ review
   your goals
   on a daily basis

< 36 >

Over the years I have noticed that successful software engineers review their goals on a daily basis. This ritual of constant review is critical, because it forces you to align every decision you make during the day with your major goals. Further, it allows you to break down each goal into smaller, executable steps. Breaking down the plan into individual tasks for the day becomes a fine-grained action plan to reach your goal - a roadmap and compass you can use to navigate towards your destination - one step at a time, though always moving in the right direction.

Keep a Log Book

It's one thing to write down your goals, but it's another to also record and monitor your progress along the way. Casually recording your progress in the random access memory of your brain allows for only minimal tracking. Instead, make your progress explicit by keeping a log. This enables you to understand what you want more clearly and to gain control of your actions. Where your attention goes, results will show up.

Very similar to a software system that logs what actions were executed, a log book records what you have accomplished every day. Indeed, I've observed that the most successful engineers take this one step further: every evening they log their accomplishments of the day and additionally create a clear list of what they want to achieve the next day. This can be as simple as three bullet points listing their highest priority tasks.

Needless to say, those three bullet points are aligned with their overall goals. Their last task of the day is to write down and log what they have accomplished today and what they want to achieve the next day. Simple, but extremely powerful. The unique power of logging comes from building up your confidence in yourself, every day. Why? Because it provides clarity, eliminates the noise, and helps you create and shape your self-identity.

>_ logging
   your accomplishments
   allows to shape
   self-identity

< 38 >

Another positive effect of keeping a log book is that it makes it easier to focus on what your goals really are. Of course, not every day is the same. Making progress does not mean you make big steps towards your goal every single day.

However, keeping a log allows you to get up again in case you fall down. When things seem overwhelming, successful software engineers skim their logs and read about past accomplishments and victories.

This helps them to keep going and to remind themselves what they already have accomplished. It shows them that this day is probably just a minor hiccup given the obstacles they have already overcome in the past.

< 40 >

successful
software
 engineers

// write down
   their goals,
   continuously
   review them, and
   log their progress
   to remain focused
   on what they
   really want

< 42 >

CHAPTER 2

Make Every Minute Count

»The key is in not spending time, but in investing it.« – Stephen R. Covey

Every morning, as soon as you wake up, your timer for the day starts to tick. Like an hourglass, one grain of sand after the other falls from the upper chamber to the lower chamber. Unstoppable.

Every passing minute chips away at the most precious resource you have: time. After that minute has passed, it's gone for good and it will never come back. No matter how hard you try, you cannot change the course of time. What you »can« change, however, is how you use the limited time you have.

< 43 >

It is totally up to you what you make of your time, you can let it pass or make it count. Consciously allocating your time, squeezing value out of every minute of the day and utilizing it effectively, will bring you closer to your goals.

>_ do not
   waste your time
   but
   make it count

Become Aware of Your Time Allocation

Let's start with a thought experiment: What if I tell you that your built-in processor can execute only a single task every day? One task, not two or three, just one. What would that task be for you today? The task that truly makes a difference and moves you closer to what you want to achieve in your life and your career?

The point here is not to limit you to one task a day, but to shift your thinking towards a mental model in which

< 44 >

you honestly and critically evaluate how you approach your day. Be honest with yourself and make a conscious decision about how to invest your time and energy every single day. Yes, you yourself decide - not your manager, not your scrum master, not a kanban board, not a backlog of bugs or features - but you.

The first lesson is to become aware of how you structure your day and how you spend your time. On the road to success, it's crucial to build an understanding of how you spend your time and how you employ your energy. The action item here is not merely to think about how you allocate your time for the day or even week. No, instead of just processing it implicitly within your memory, you need to make that information explicit. Making implicit information explicit is the key to increasing the impact of every day of your life.

>_ become aware
of your
time allocation

< 45 >

Here is a pragmatic suggestion: for the next seven days, write down how you spend your time and record it in a spreadsheet. If you spend time messaging back and forth with your friends through an instant messenger, write it down. If you spend time on social media, write it down. If you brew 18 cups of coffee throughout the day, write it down. All these tasks consume time and hence take time away from more important things you could be doing.

Seven days from now, take the spreadsheet and generate a chart of your time usage. It's an insightful self-evaluation lesson when you sit down with a fresh cup of coffee or tea and stare at that donut or pie chart. The funny thing is, your mind plays tricks on you - it's very likely that the way you think you invest your time doesn't match what the chart reflects. Be assured, if you've kept accurate records then the chart will not lie to you.

I do this exercise with every single one of my clients in my highly individualized coaching engagements. Literally all of my clients report it's an eye opening experience to actually see and evaluate how they invest their time. The most common reaction when engineers stare at a chart that reflects their time allocation is: »I had no idea that Task X and Task Y consume so much of my time.«

Remember, being busy does not mean you are being

< 46 >

productive. Hence, the simplest way to transition into a more conscious time allocation is to schedule check-ins with yourself throughout the day and ask: »Is the task I am doing right now a task that brings me closer to my goals?« This practice will make you more aware of how you invest your time and help you understand if your tasks are aligned with what you want to achieve.

>_ being busy does not mean you are being productive

What You Can Change and What You Can't

There are certain facts that we simply cannot change. The best way to deal with such facts is to accept them and not invest time and energy in trying to change them. It's a losing battle and distracts you from things that move you toward your destination.

< 47 >

Here's an example. Let's say you drop your laptop and it bursts into a million pieces. As unfortunate and regrettable as it is, no matter how much you beat yourself up, nothing will put your computer back together. Once the harm is done, it's done. At this point you have two options: either you wallow in self-pity, or you accept the fact that it's broken and direct your gaze forward.

Time invested in trying to change things that you can't change is a waste of your mental energy. You are better off accepting those facts and understanding the difference between the things you can and the things you can't change.

I recently heard one of my clients say: »If I were born in a different country, I would already be successful.« Even though I understand that some people struggle with geographical disadvantages, you simply cannot change the country you were born in. Another client said: »Easy for him to say, his parents were rich and allowed him to attend the most prestigious engineering school.«

Every minute you devote to such thoughts takes time away from the important things you should be doing. You can't change the country you were born in, your parents, and a thousand other things that could fill a book bigger

< 48 >

than this one. In fact, the only thing you can change is your attitude. There's an old saying: before you judge the world, set your own house in order. Your engineering life will take a dramatic turn for the better once you jump into the driver's seat and focus on the things that you can change instead of constantly getting upset about things you have no control over.

>_ don't devote a single minute to things you can't control

The Best Hour of the Day

You've probably heard the joke that there are two kinds of people in the world: those who think there are two kinds of people in the world, and those who don't. Well, even if there aren't only two kinds of people in the world, there are certainly only two kinds of tasks in your day: reactive and proactive.

< 49 >

Reactive tasks are triggered by an outside stimulus, which initiates an action you then most likely execute.

Proactive tasks are triggered by your intrinsic motivation or what we can think of as an inside stimulus, which initiates an action you would like to accomplish.

Both reactive and proactive tasks are part of our daily routine, but completing the proactive tasks is commonly harder than the other way around. The reason is that proactive tasks are generally easier to postpone, whereas reactive tasks usually require instant action.

Let's take a look at a simplified example. Imagine you are crafting a proposal for a code refactor (proactive) when your boss informs you about a new security incident (reactive). You instantly drop working on your proposal and help your boss put out the fire. Inevitably, reactive tasks take precedence over proactive tasks. Thus the proactive task, in this case writing the proposal, will be postponed.

The longer you wait on any given day to complete a proactive task, the harder it will be to get it done because more and more reactive tasks will crop up (email messages, last-minute meetings, urgent bug fixes, etc.). Hence, let me

< 50 >

introduce you to a concept that has proved very rewarding among successful software engineers.

Recall the question from the beginning of this chapter: if there is only one task that I can accomplish today, what would it be? The key is to make that task the very first thing you do in the morning, even before you check your email, log into a bug tracker, or attend your first meeting. Give yourself the best hour of the day and deeply focus on your most important proactive task for one hour.

>_ claim
   the best hour
   of the day
   for yourself

During that best hour of the day you are mentally fresh. More importantly, it doesn't matter what reactive tasks you have to take on after that, because you have already made progress on your most important task. The one that actual-

< 51 >

ly moves you closer to your goals. Remember, consistency is key, and you will feel a sense of accomplishment every day when you make progress on your most important task.

Automate, Automate, Automate

As a software engineer you are faced with tackling a multitude of recurring tasks each and every day. Examples are checking for reported problems through a ticketing system and monitoring critical performance metrics. Point is, those recurring tasks eat up time you could spend more productively. In economics, this loss of other alternatives is called opportunity cost. You are missing out on opportunities when you invest significant time in recurring tasks.

Successful engineers always look for opportunities to automate recurring tasks. They perform a quick return of investment analysis, which is an approximate measure of an investment's profitability, and then invest the time to craft scripts that will allow them to automate those recurring tasks.

Use your favorite scripting language to craft code that supports you throughout the day. Basically these scripts al-

< 52 >

low you to delegate the tasks that consume your precious time but are not worth focusing on every day. You can see every script as a »success fighter« that defends your time and schedule. Every single script in your success army then fights to defend your time so you can accomplish your goals more quickly and effectively.

>_ look for opportunities to automate recurring tasks

Saying No is a Skill

Remember, your energy is finite, so choose wisely how you use it. Once you become aware of how precious your time is, you become really careful about how you invest it.

Success does not come from taking on everything that comes your way. Rather it comes from focusing on a few

< 53 >

things that really matter and doing them extremely well. Say yes to what matters, and allow yourself to say no to the things that don't matter. Put bluntly, take on less, accomplish more. Your time is an asset that needs to be cherished and guarded.

Instead of blindly executing, think twice how you allocate your time. Going forward, you will see that you won't work hard to be busy, but work smart to have an impact. Ultimately, making conscious decisions about how you spend your time will help turbocharge your path to success.

>_ success comes from
focusing
on a few things
that really matter

< 54 >

successful
software
engineers

// use every minute
wisely to
make progress
toward their
major goals

< 56 >

CHAPTER 3

Cultivate Your Communication

»Communication is not about speaking what we think. Communication is about ensuring others hear what we mean.«
— Simon Sinek

Thinking clearly and expressing yourself clearly can have a massive impact on your career. These essential skills help you gain support for your initiatives, avoid conflict, and strengthen rapport with your colleagues, teammates, and customers. They even increase your self-awareness so that you can work more effectively on your own tasks and projects. Plain and simple, having profound communication skills will increase your impact, your visibility, and how you are perceived - producing positive results in all aspects of your work.

< 57 >

In essence all of our communication happens on three levels: (a) Writing, (b) Speaking, and (c) Listening. In this chapter we'll dive into all three, so let's get started.

>_ clear communication enables you to win people over to your side

Cultivate Your Writing

First and foremost, good writing takes time and practice. Absolutely no proposal, blog post, newsletter, report, statement, briefing, design document, research paper, or any other sort of document should be published without enough time to perform iterative edits and improvements.

A confusing, poorly written, and badly structured text will immediately draw the attention of every reader - and not in a good way.

< 58 >

Not only will it harm your reputation, but if readers need to put in too much effort then you won't win anyone over to your side.

Let me exaggerate to emphasize my point. If you need to send out a briefing that will be read by 300 people, then you should be the one putting in 300 minutes (5 hours!) or more so that it takes each reader only one minute to understand your point. It should never be the other way around. You should never be the one taking the easy route. Your job is to make things easy for the reader, not yourself.

In reverse, if you don't put in the effort then it might take each of those 300 people 5 hours to understand the point you are making. Think about it from your own perspective: if a briefing demanded 5 hours of your precious time, then you would quickly give up.

On the other hand, if you can instantly capture the interest of your reader, if you manage to get them engaged in your captivating briefing, then it is more likely they will follow you along and you can win their support.

< 59 >

>_ good writing pays dividends throughout your career

Here are some tips and techniques for crafting a profound and persuasive document.

First, have a clearly defined message, which starts with a clear and self-explanatory title. If needed, add further information like a subtitle, date, and author. Sounds obvious, right? Indeed it is, but I have seen so many documents that fail right from the beginning.

Second, start at a high level and add more details as you go along. As we know, time is a precious resource and not all of your readers need all the details. Ask yourself: What high level information can I provide in the beginning so that the reader will quickly get what they need? This key information is often called an executive summary, but it's not just for executives! Needless to say, you must back up

< 60 >

your high level explanation with details and facts further down in the text.

Third, carefully evaluate what is most important to mention - and what is not. Make sure you have a sound and consistent story. If a statement does not really support your argumentation, leave it out. No one minds not reading what is not important. Eliminate filling sentences and only keep words that express what you actually want to get across.

Fourth, guide and support the reader by letting them know what to think. You do this by eliminating any room for speculation and interpretation in your writing. Remove words that mean something different for every reader. Let's look at an illustrative example: »By removing unused code we drastically improve performance.« What does that mean to you? To me, »drastically« translates to an 80% performance win, while for someone else it could mean 20%. Avoid words and phrases that allow for speculation. Instead, be as precise as possible and quantify what you actually mean.

Fifth, keep the reader engaged and entertained. Good documents use active voice instead of passive voice. Active voice costs the reader so much less energy to read and to digest your message. Don't repeat words and phrases. Instead, find words that better describe and express what you actually want to say. If needed, get assistance by finding synonyms for related concepts. Pro tip: all modern editors have plugins (such as a thesaurus) that can help you craft convincing documents.

Obviously the above suggestions are only a small excerpt of what it takes to craft a solid document. The most important point is to shift your mindset and realize that cultivating your writing can help you enhance your influence and reputation. Simply by following the foregoing tips, you already have the basics of powerful writing covered. Practice good writing because it's a skill that pays dividends time after time.

Cultivate Your Speaking

As with good writing, public speaking is a skill that will serve you throughout your entire career. Public speaking does not necessarily mean that you have to be on stage and

< 62 >

give a talk, though to be really successful you should aim for becoming confident on stage. No, public speaking starts somewhere else. In fact, every water cooler conversation and coffee chat you have is a kind of public speaking. It is part of every one-on-one, and of every team meeting.

>_ the sooner you
   start practicing,
   the longer
   you can benefit
   from public
   speaking skills

Successful people use every opportunity to improve their speaking and they always prepare for such events. They do not randomly walk into a meeting and see what happens. They prepare and oftentimes even rehearse what they are going to say. They prepare their positions and the points they want to get across. They know that it's not how good

< 63 >

you are, but it's how good you want to be. It's about how you want to be perceived - and solid speaking skills make you appear professional. It's also about building empathy and establishing trust, which help to create and shape relationships.

Before I provide some practical tips, I want to share a dilemma that causes most of the problems in our day-to-day communication. It's called the »Sender-Receiver Problem« and it's probably the biggest obstacle we face when we communicate with each other. You say something, but the other person interprets it in a completely different way than you intended.

Fact is, we all process information differently. We receive and decode information based on our background, culture, social class, and prior knowledge of the topic. Whatever seems polite or rude to you, can be processed completely differently by the receiver. It's important to be aware of this dilemma when communicating with someone, because it has a massive impact on the outcome of the conversation. The best tip I have is to be clear and use language that every person understands. In addition, try to »read the room« and learn to listen (more on that below).

< 64 >

Here are some tips and techniques for improving your public speaking and giving better presentations.

First and foremost, it's not about you, it's about your audience. Ask yourself, what do you want your audience to know and get out of your talk? Stop worrying about yourself and how you are perceived. Instead, start focusing on the value you give the audience. When you do so, you'll realize that people in the audience will also perceive that value - and perceive you as valuable.

Second, don't drown your audience in data. Use data points to deliver a key message but eliminate everything that does not clearly support your purpose. Reducing and eliminating noise from your story, and your slides, allows your audience to follow you where you want to lead them. It also keeps them engaged, because they don't get side-tracked or overwhelmed with information that is not useful or on point.

Third, if you want to keep your audience engaged, start strong and speak slowly. People who feel they are not worthy of being listened to tend to talk too fast. You have something to say, so ensure you are not rushing. The best

< 65 >

way to do this is by memorizing your introduction. In fact, it is just as important to memorize your conclusion, since the beginning and the end are the most important parts of your talk.

As with every other key career skill, public speaking cannot be learned in a day. Thankfully, there are lots and lots of opportunities to practice. Practice in front of a mirror, record yourself, watch and study yourself. Find a mentor with whom to practice. Take every opportunity to practice your public speaking in front of real people. The more you practice, the more natural it will feel to you. And the sooner you start practicing, the longer you can benefit from great public speaking skills.

Cultivate Your Listening

Although we communicate constantly, paradoxically it seems that the fundamentals of conversation have stopped working. Most people believe that speaking is the only skill that matters for better conversations, but that is not true. To effectively communicate your ideas, you also need to master the art of listening well.

< 66 >

>_ give your conversation partner your full attention

Genuine, honest, and sincere listening is a highly underrated skill. When in conversations, most people already formulate their answers in their head while the other person is still speaking. That's not listening.

Successful people give the person they are listening to their most valuable gift: their attention. Spend time getting to know your conversation partners and understanding their needs and goals instead of putting yourself first. You can only influence and win someone over if you understand and care about their needs, goals, and priorities.

The Stoic philosopher Epictetus put it this way: we have two ears and one mouth so that we can listen twice as much as we speak. Speaking only allows you to repeat what you already know. Only if you listen carefully will you learn something new. And even though you might think you already know a lot, everyone you talk to knows something that you do not.

< 67 >

Start to practice your listening and really try to understand what the other person is telling you. When in a conversation, do not multitask. When you're listening to someone, give that person your full focus. Let the conversation and the other party be the center of your attention.

In summary, practice your writing, speaking, and listening. Successful people know the importance of those tools and use all three, all the time.

< 68 >

successful
software
engineers

// cultivate their
communication
so they can
influence
the people
around them
and clearly convey
their goals
and vision

Beyond the Code

< 70 >

CHAPTER 4

Create
Solutions

»Do not blame the world.
Find a solution.« – Sri Chinmoy

The message of this chapter is quite simple:

»Don't identify problems, but create solutions.« Paradoxically, when you focus on problems instead of solutions, all you do is create more problems. More precisely, when you constantly look out for problems, more and more obstacles will appear on the horizon and success will fade away. By contrast, when you focus on creating solutions, you will see endless opportunities and possibilities. This empowers you to search for solutions - and finding solutions translates to success.

< 71 >

Thankfully, it's up to you whether you'll live in a world of problems or a world of opportunities. It's an inner state of how you view the world and you can make a conscious decision about that inner state. You have the ability to shift your focus and to see possibilities everywhere you look. Successful people know that by being positive - more precisely, by »choosing to be positive« - you open so many doors and set yourself up to enjoy the process as well as the success.

>_ finding and creating solutions translates to success

Evaluate What Needs a Solution

It's one thing to know that you should create solutions. It's another to know which problems to solve. Yes, even though you need to focus on creating solutions, every

< 72 >

compelling solution begins with an important problem to be solved. After all, you don't want to create a solution in search of a problem!

Successful engineers don't just identify problems, but instead they actually solve those problems. No one will think you are incredibly smart and productive, or promote you to positions of greater responsibility, if all you can do is point out problems. It's rather the opposite: no one wants to be around someone whose only contribution is negative. In our everyday life this is comparable to people who are constantly complaining about what bad shape the world is in. Those people are never the successful ones, who instead are busy coming up with solutions to change the world for the better.

Moreover, successful engineers know they can't fix all the problems, so they concentrate on identifying the most important problems where they can have the biggest impact. They have internalized that they can only change so much and thus they are careful about choosing what problems to work on. They have also realized that fixing problems with low impact does not help them accelerate their career advancement.

< 73 >

>_ you are defined by the solutions you create; choose wisely

Successful engineers have a value system that guides them to select the highest impact problems. This value system is also an intelligent, subtle, and efficient delegation mechanism, because it lets someone else handle low-impact problems.

Finally, successful engineers carefully select the problems by which they will be defined. If you only fix small problems that only have low impact, then you will be perceived as a low-impact person. If, however, you solve big problems, you will be recognized as a high-impact person and your career will blossom.

Always keep this mind: the problems you select and solve will define who you are.

< 74 >

How to Create Solutions

Stop focusing on what is broken, and start focusing on what you can build. Ask yourself: What am I in control of? What can I do better? How can I improve things? A problem-solving mindset will help you move past roadblocks much faster.

>_ put a price tag on your solution

Here are a few pragmatic tips that will guide you to intelligently creating solutions.

First, start by defining the problem as precisely as possible. Write down a problem statement which accurately captures the problem. Make sure that you explicitly state the benefits of solving this problem for all the stakeholders involved. If possible, quantify the value of your solution by specifying these benefits in monetary terms, such as savings realized or sales increased.

< 75 >

Second, identify not just one possible solution, but provide a list of alternatives. Explicitly identifying and evaluating alternative approaches helps you avoid settling too quickly on a particular approach that might not be the best.

Third, choose the best solution. Write down why it is the best solution and advocate for it by preparing a case. Ideally back up your thinking with data explaining why the chosen solution is the best way to fix the problem.

Fourth, ensure that your solution is realistic by defining a plan to make it happen. What resources will you need? What are the inputs and outputs? What are potential blockers? What are the key milestones?

Fifth, start to implement the solution and keep track of your progress. Carefully record the advancements you are making. As we have learned, it's best to document your work in a log book.

Sixth, once you have fixed the problem, evaluate how you did so. Write down what you learned, what worked well, and ways to improve when tackling a similar problem in the future.

< 76 >

Remember, you want to create solutions that have a massive impact and bring big rewards. Fixing a massive problem and creating a solution for it can occasionally feel overwhelming. Sometimes you might even think that you want to give up, but there is an easy mind trick that enables you to tackle big problems yet still remain on track.

One Bite at a Time

Have you ever heard the question »How do you eat an elephant?« Seems impossible, right? When you think about it, an adult male elephant weighs up to 7 tons (14,000 lb). When knowing the weight you are probably tempted to give up before you have even started. Besides the fact that an elephant might not even taste that good.

What the question really asks is: how do you succeed at a large, complex, time-consuming project that seems impossible at first? The most common answer to the elephant question is »One bite at a time.« Meaning, take one bite, put your focus only on that one bite, do not look at the entire elephant, and then take another bite.

< 77 >

>_ focus on the current task and let your future self worry about future obstacles

Let's translate the above into a more concrete action statement. In essence, start by doing what you can, what is possible. Focus on the next step and do the next task well. Don't try to overcome a future obstacle that is far in the future and not even well defined at this point. Then simply rinse and repeat. Pretty soon you realize that you are about to accomplish what seemed impossible at first.

This strategy has proven itself countless times. A successful engineer once shared the following story with me: Our team had to re-architect our entire application. The single process architecture was outdated and there was no way we could continue maintaining it. After the first few meetings, we realized we had to climb a massive wall of design changes to re-architect the system. Instead of focusing on the complex end goal, we started to shift our focus

< 78 >

on one step at a time and we were able to slowly but sure-ly solve the problem. This way of thinking is also a great motivational tool. Why? Because motivation comes from being in motion. Once you have accomplished one task, you feel like you can accomplish another and another till you have finally created a solution for the big complex task.

Take Risks

Creating solutions inevitably means taking risks. You'll never create viable solutions if you're not willing to take risks. The positive effect of taking risks is that it will ignite a growth process within yourself as well. Taking risks is a sign of your commitment to creating solutions. It shows that you can make a decision and stand behind it. In turn, taking risks will make you stronger, braver, and build your confidence in yourself and your abilities.

At this point it's important to point out the difference between taking risks and gambling. When you take a cal-culated risk, you make an informed, educated guess about what's necessary to solve the problem. When you gamble, you are careless about the costs, consequences, or results of your decision. Moreover, taking calculated risks goes hand in hand with taking one bite at a time. Together, these methods help you build up the muscle and the will necessary to move faster and faster toward your solution.

Here is a pragmatic suggestion: Don't be shy! Be bold and believe in yourself. You will not achieve great success if you constantly wait for the perfect moment to act. Dare to take risks and take full responsibility for your decisions. If things go wrong you can always ask for forgiveness later, but if you never take risks you will never succeed.

>_ taking risks will build confidence in yourself and your abilities

Taking a risk means taking a chance, using an opportunity to try something new. Obviously taking a chance entails the risk of failing, but also the possibility of success. Successful people know that if you want to advance then you eventually must take your chances. Taking a chance is crucial and of uttermost importance to advance your skills, gain experience, and become truly successful. Besides, if you wait too long, someone else might come along and solve the problem before you do!

< 80 >

successful
software
engineers

// focus on creating
solutions
instead of
identifying
problems and take
calculated risks
to accomplish
their goals

< 82 >

CHAPTER 5

Own
Your
Mistakes

*»The only man who never makes a mistake
is the man who never does anything.«* – Theodore Roosevelt

To give you some peace of mind, let's be clear from the start that it's completely natural to have negative feelings about mistakes and failures. After all, you tried something and it didn't work out as you wanted. Failing at something is obviously a painful experience. It simply hurts.

However, seeing mistakes as purely negative is valid only if you consider a narrow time span. In the long run, the opposite turns out to be true: namely, mistakes are positive. They make you stronger. They provide fertile soil to

< 83 >

grow new skills. Ultimately, they help you become more successful as a software engineer.

>_ mistakes make you stronger

Many people, when making a mistake, instantly give up. They say to themselves that they can't do it. They think they are a failure. Even worse, they start to believe that they can't become successful because of the mistakes they are making. This is exactly the misconception that I want you to understand so that you can flush it out of your mental cache. In short, the most important message I want to get across in this chapter is that you should never, ever give up because you made a mistake.

Mistakes Build the Foundation

It's critical to understand and to page into your sub-conscious mind that mistakes are not the opposite of suc-

< 84 >

cess. Mistakes build the foundation for success to happen at all. It's easy to never make a mistake: never try anything new, just stand still and do nothing at all to advance your career. But rest assured, if you don't try, if you never even make an attempt to follow through on your aspirations, then you will also not achieve anything substantial in your engineering life. In fact, the biggest mistake is trying to avoid mistakes.

>_ never ever
   give up
   because
   you made a mistake

Sure, mistakes are a painful experience, but the truth is that our toughest failures correlate directly with the most transformative moments of growth. A lot of engineers who come to my coaching sessions are scared, even frightened of failure and mistakes. They are sometimes so scared of making mistakes that they put off going after what they really want. If you worry too much about exposing yourself,

< 85 >

if you worry too much about failing and making mistakes, then I can guarantee you that you will never be truly successful. The fear of failure and making mistakes has killed more dreams than actually making the mistake ever will.

As we established in the last chapter, success comes from solving problems and creating solutions for those problems. If you don't try to create solutions then you will never solve any problems and in turn will never become successful. Trying and failing, modifying your approach, trying and failing again, never giving up, learning from the mistakes, and trying again and again - this is the crucial cycle of growing and becoming more successful as a software engineer.

Don't be scared of mistakes, and don't view mistakes as a negative, but rather see them for what they are: part of the process. Mistakes teach you what doesn't work and encourage you to create and develop new ways of thinking and doing. This shift in mindset frees up positive energy for improving your skills and expanding your expertise.

Probably you have heard the saying: an expert is someone who has made all the possible mistakes in a narrow

< 86 >

field. And it's true: you cannot become an expert if you try to avoid mistakes.

Don't Try To Avoid Mistakes

Two keys to career advancement are setting high standards for yourself and proactively working toward your goals. However, being obsessed with perfection and trying to avoid mistakes will take you off course. Don't strive for perfection, because perfection easily gets in the way and it might even become a barrier to growth. Don't get me wrong, striving for excellence is a great motivational tool, but holding yourself to impossibly high standards can cause you to strive for ideals which are unattainable.

>_ you cannot
   become an expert
   if you try
   to avoid mistakes

< 87 >

From an emotional point of view you will start to feel as if you are never good enough. This will take energy away from your work and detract from your effectiveness.

For example, trying to write utterly flawless code is a fool's errand, because we know that all code has bugs. But that shouldn't hold you back from publishing your code and shipping your software.

More generally, when you try to be perfect you limit your ability to contribute to big projects and big goals. As a result, you'll never be recognized for what you can truly accomplish. Furthermore, if you don't admit to and own your mistakes, you won't discover what you've missed, what went wrong and where you can improve. Of course, striving to do great work is important to become successful. But if you carry it too far and believe you need to be perfect, sooner or later you will stagnate and you won't harvest the fruits of your hard work.

Remember, no person is perfect. Know when enough is enough and allow yourself to be satisfied with delivering results where you performed well. Sure, it won't be flawless, but what is? Doing good work is obviously better than waiting to release your work until it's perfect, because it

< 88 >

never will be. As the saying goes: the perfect is the enemy of the good. Get comfortable with incremental improvements over time and your career will benefit from continuous learning.

>_ get comfortable with incremental improvements

What You Can Learn From Your Mistakes

Learning from your mistakes as a software engineer sets the stage for personal and professional growth, and it benefits both you and your team. Here are some pragmatic reasons why your mistakes allow you to grow.

First, by acknowledging your mistakes, you open up opportunities for learning. Reflecting on what went wrong helps you understand what caused the error and how to avoid it in the future, continually making you a better software engineer over time.

< 89 >

Second, taking responsibility for your mistakes shows honesty and integrity. It demonstrates that you are reliable and trustworthy, even when things go wrong. This is extremely important, because trust is critical in any team environment.

Third, when you own your mistakes, it encourages others to do the same. This creates a culture where team members are not afraid to admit errors, making it easier to quickly identify and resolve issues collectively.

Fourth, professionals who are willing to acknowledge and learn from their mistakes are respected and valued. Colleagues and team members recognize the importance of continuous improvement, and owning mistakes showcases your commitment to follow through on your principles.

Fifth, taking responsibility for your mistakes demonstrates accountability. It shows that you are aware of your actions and are willing to face the consequences. This mindset is not only crucial for personal development and professional success, but fosters a culture of accountability in your team.

< 90 >

Remember, everyone makes mistakes, and it's a natural part of the software development lifecycle.

Make Better Decisions in the Future

When you talk with people who are immensely successful (and I encourage you to do so!), they will all confirm a powerful truth: the most painful mistakes are the ones that teach you the most and enable you to make better decisions in the future.

In every walk of life, successful people do not fear mistakes. They don't blame someone else for their failures and mistakes. Instead, they take full responsibility for their actions and claim ownership of their mistakes. They internalize the pain and use that grief to ensure they will make better decisions in the future.

What truly matters is how you handle those mistakes and what you do to prevent similar issues in the future. Embrace your mistakes as opportunities for growth and improvement, and you'll become a more skilled and valued software engineer in the long run.

< 91 >

When I hear an engineer say »this is my fault« then I know that they are onto something big. Using a phrase like this signals that you take full responsibility and claim ownership of the mistake. This means you are someone who doesn't fear failure but instead uses failure to learn and grow.

The key is: don't give mistakes the power to dominate you or allow them to hold you back. Remember: mistakes only make you stronger.

```
>_ the less afraid
   you are of making
   mistakes
   the faster
   you will grow
```

Keep creating, keep learning, keep making mistakes. The less afraid you are of making mistakes, the faster you will grow.

< 92 >

Keep calm, focus on resilience and always look at the situation optimistically. Start to analyze your values rather than your fears. This way of thinking will provide confidence, security, a sense of well being, and the ability to contribute at a higher level.

Be the best version of yourself every day. No matter what you are working towards, doing it to the best of your abilities brings great rewards. When you do your best, you do it with the intention to succeed.

Remain optimistic and never give up. Mistakes are not the opposite of success. Instead, they are a necessary ingredient of success. Only by being open to making mistakes will you create an engineering life full of achievement, passion, and fulfillment.

< 93 >

< 94 >

successful
software
engineers

// own their mistakes
and use them
to make better
decisions
in the future

< 96 >

CHAPTER 6

Seek
a
Mentor

»You cannot teach a man anything. You can only help him discover it within himself.« – Galileo Galilei

Before setting out to find a mentor, it's crucial to understand what a mentor is, how a mentor can help you on your career journey, and why you should be intentional about choosing one. Furthermore, outstanding software engineers not only have a mentor, but they also serve as a mentor and pass on their expertise and experience to others. They do so because serving as a mentor clarifies their own identity and strengthens their sense of purpose in their engineering life.

Ultimately, by both having and being a mentor you can reach your goals more quickly and accelerate your path to success.

Your Ideal Mentor

Your ideal mentor has traveled the path that you are on right now. The only difference is that they are ahead of you on that path. Your mentor is already where you want to be five, ten, even twenty years from now. Equally important, a mentor is a role model for you because they exhibit positive behaviors that you want to emulate.

Here's an example to illustrate the point. Let's say you've decided to climb Nanga Parbat, an immense mountain in the Himalayas which is extremely difficult to climb. It's a strenuous ascent to reach the summit and even very experienced mountaineers have given up somewhere along the way. Some have even lost their lives attempting to reach the top of this mountain, which is among the highest on earth.

To increase your chances of reaching the summit, would you ask for advice from someone who has not successfully climbed the mountain? Even worse, would you trust

< 98 >

someone who claims to know everything about high altitude mountaineering because they have read two books and watched a few documentaries about it? Surely not! You wouldn't put your life in the hands of any random person. Instead, you would seek out someone who has extensive experience in the Himalayas and ideally someone who has been to the top of Nanga Parbat.

>_ choose a mentor who already is where you want to be

As you see, an appropriate mentor needs to be someone who has established a certain level of credibility and has already achieved what you want to achieve in your life and career. Your mentor needs to be someone you look up to, someone you trust, and someone who can guide you on the path to achieving your goals.

< 99 >

The Benefits of Having a Mentor

The great thing about having a mentor is that it enables you to accelerate not only your professional development, but also your personal development. There are several key areas where a mentor can be critically important to your success.

The first is goals. Here a mentor can help you set ambitious but realistic goals, motivate you to stay on track, and hold you accountable.

The second is decision-making. Your mentor doesn't make decisions for you, but gently guides you to finding the right course of action on your own.

The third is perspective. A strong mentor encourages you to ignore the noise and invest your energy where it really moves you forward.

The fourth is handling ambiguous situations. A good mentor is able to provide valuable advice regarding office politics, skills you need to develop, new opportunities, and your promotion path.

< 100 >

>_ a great mentor holds you accountable but is also your greatest supporter

A good mentor is by your side even when things get tough and understands that you have to be persistent to become truly successful. A mentor is also a fan and supporter of yours, who lifts you up and celebrates your victories and achievements with you.

Without a mentor, negative thoughts may become more prominent in your daily life, especially when dealing with challenging subjects such as a difficult boss or an unclear path to promotion.

With a good mentor, however, you can transform whatever makes you feel uncomfortable into something posi-

< 101 >

tive, because a good mentor knows that discomfort quite often comes from a fear of change.

Your mentor listens to your fears with compassion, but encourages you to overcome them and to take concrete action in the face of uncertainty.

Your mentor has probably made some of the mistakes you have, and can share valuable lessons on how to use them to come closer to your goals - one step at a time.

A smart engineer learns from their own mistakes, but a truly wise engineer learns from the mistakes of others, too.

```
>_ a wise engineer
   learns from their
   own mistakes, but
   also from those
   of others
```

< 102 >

Finding a Mentor

First, don't rush into selecting a mentor just so you can say you have one. It's important to take your time and carefully select the person you want to give your trust and from whom you want to receive advice and guidance. There are lots of people out there who are disguised as a mentor but might not have your best interest at heart.

> \>_ do not take advice
>   from people
>   who are not
>   where you want to be

If you ask the wrong people for advice and mentorship, they could unknowingly or even knowingly guide you in the wrong direction without you even realizing it. Most people instantly have an opinion when you ask them, especially when you ask them for advice. They seemingly always have the best advice for someone else's situation. But you

< 103 >

should take advice only from people you actually trust and admire.

Let me be clear: there is nothing wrong with gathering as much information as possible so you can make better, well-informed decisions for your career path. What I want you to realize is that you should not necessarily listen to the advice given by random people. Most important: don't take advice from someone who is not where you want to be.

It might sound like your mentor needs to be close to perfect, but don't get discouraged. Finding a mentor is also not rocket science. Just open your eyes and look for people who have already accomplished what you would like to accomplish. Keep your eye out for someone you look up to and can trust. There is a saying: once the student is ready, the right teacher will appear.

Once you have identified a person, it's OK to simply ask them if they might want to be your mentor. What's the worst thing that can happen? They can say no. But if you don't ask, then the answer will always be no! More often than not, people who are successful are willing to share

< 104 >

their wisdom and insights with a less experienced colleague. And someone who doesn't want to give back isn't someone you want to work with, anyway. I have mentored a lot of engineers throughout the years and I have always felt flattered when upcoming talents seek my advice, help, and mentorship.

Meeting with Your Mentor

The duration and consistency of each mentoring relationship is different, like every other relationship in life. My recommendation is that mentors and mentees should meet at least once per month. Maybe twice a month in the beginning because, as with every other relationship, it takes time to bond and build rapport. Once you have established a certain level of trust and commitment with your mentor, you can go back to meeting once a month.

What I can recommend is that you keep your mentor informed about what's happening in your work life. However, don't be overly demanding, either. Your mentor's time is precious and it's important to respect that. Don't spam your mentor with daily updates, but

< 105 >

keep your mentor informed about how your career is progressing. Generally, it's ideal to schedule a standing meeting to check in monthly, for instance at 10:00am on the first Tuesday of the month. After all, you want your mentor to provide technical as well as emotional guidance on how to take appropriate action. In my experience, that works best if you meet at a regular cadence.

The Power of Being a Mentor

Successful software engineers choose to help others because they understand the value of their wisdom and knowledge, and they want to pass it on. They also enjoy the challenge of guiding upcoming and motivated individuals through the learning process so they can reach their goals.

>_ being a mentor
   brings out
   the best in you
   and forces you to
   act as a role model

< 106 >

More importantly, they know that being a mentor requires them to act as a role model and to live up to their personal and professional standards. And, in turn, acting as a role model forces them to hold themselves accountable and even helps them become more successful, too.

Those who advance the right way understand that success isn't only a matter of taking but also of giving. They know that they are fortunate and they make a conscious decision to help others, because by helping others they help themselves. In fact, helping others will strengthen your sense of purpose in your life and your career. No matter where you are in your career, you can always help someone who is more junior than you to advance and grow as an engineer and as a person.

< 107 >

< 108 >

successful
software
engineers

// work with a mentor
to accelerate
their development
and serve as
a mentor
to reinforce
their best self

< 110 >

CHAPTER 7

Nourish Your Environment

*»Wherever there is a human being,
there is an opportunity for kindness.« – Seneca*

To change, improve, grow, and become truly successful, you need to realize that you cannot do it alone. Support and help the people around you so they can grow and thrive, too. To some of my clients, this way of thinking seems counterintuitive. Unfortunately, they have been programmed to believe that every game can have only one winner - and that if someone else is successful, it eliminates their chances of doing the same. Thankfully, that is simply not true. In fact, I have observed the opposite: namely, success compounds. Your success does not eliminate oth-

< 111 >

er people's chances of success. Success is not a zero-sum game. You can be successful and have an impact while simultaneously the engineers around you, your peers, and your friends can be vastly successful too.

>_ success is not a zero-sum game; success compounds

Nourish your environment and your environment will nourish you. True and lasting success is a symbiosis where all parties benefit from the relationship.

Once you understand that you cannot do it alone and you have established that »collective we« within you, you will realize that a supporting group of allies is critical to your success in the engineering world.

Form Allies

Especially in these days of highly complex software systems, even the most brilliant person cannot create a product all by themselves. Having a highly effective team and

< 112 >

a strong personal network is not a luxury - it is a necessity. To do this, create connections with the people around you and try to help them whenever you can. Not only in technical matters, but in all activities and even more in times of struggle. Think about it: if you give a helping hand to someone in need, then surely that someone will be willing to support and help you in return.

Try to establish that network and strengthen those relationships by creating team spirit. The simplest way to start is by referring to your team as »us«.

>_ truly want
the people
around you
to succeed, too

Create an environment that nourishes every single person you work with. Join forces, form allies, and really strive to help the folks around you succeed. Other people can feel it if you truly want them to thrive and win. In turn, they

< 113 >

will want the best for you, as well.

It's truly amazing to observe when engineers form allies and start to build a supportive community. Such an environment enables each individual to grow at the maximum speed possible and soon they operate on a completely different level. When you are surrounded by smart people who are capable of doing outstanding things, you benefit from their skills and grow much faster.

>_ start operating in a collective we-mode

Adapting this way of thinking and starting to operate in »a collective we-mode« fosters strong allies because you all work in your collective best interest.

< 114 >

Have Empathy

Successful engineers know that we are good at programming machines, but we ourselves are not machines. We are human beings and, as such, we need to cultivate the ability to understand and care for each other. We need to make an effort to understand other people's needs, their thoughts and their point of view.

Be aware that everyone relies on a different belief system to navigate the world, based on their experience of life. Every belief system has its strengths and flaws, but surely it is finely tuned to serve the best interests of the person who relies on it.

Professionally, some engineers just got out of college, some have already been in the industry for years, and some might have an academic background. Personally, some are single, some live in a relationship, maybe with kids, and some others have to take care of their sick partner or parents.

Although you can't know the entire background of the people you work with, surely everyone has interests and

things they deeply care about besides programming com-
puters. Only if you start to value things that are important
to someone else you can truly build a relationship that lasts.
Caring about someone enables you to build rapport and
trust. And if you trust someone, you can rely on them to
help and support you in times of struggle, which benefits
you as well as your counterpart.

>_ become
a good listener
and always
be gentle

The pragmatic advice I can offer at this point is quite
simple: be gentle and bring the highest amount of respect
to the people around you. Really try to see things from the
other person's viewpoint. Become a good listener and truly
value other people and their perspectives, even - or especially - when they differ from yours.

< 116 >

Full Attention

As we've seen in the chapter »Cultivate Your Communication«, it's important to practice listening. Listening is the best way to get to know your colleagues, peers, and the people around you. A good conversation is not a one-way street - the words and understanding must flow in both directions. Indeed, a good conversation is a partnership to which you're both contributing.

When your conversation partner is speaking, it's important that you give your full attention. Listen - and listen carefully. Open your ears and your mind to what your conversation partner wants you to know. Do not instantly give them advice or start formulating your answer while the other person is speaking. This is actually hard work, and takes a fair amount of practice.

Also realize that your problems are different from their problems. You have not encountered the same problems in your life because every situation is unique. The pragmatic advice is again quite simple: listen.

< 117 >

Here is a scenario that might be familiar. You are engaged in a conversation with someone and then you hear their phone make a notification sound. Your conversation partner apparently received a text message, pulls out their phone, and says »let me check that real quick«. How does that make you feel? Even worse, what if the other person then starts furiously typing on the phone. Do you still feel you are the center of their attention?

When you're in a conversation with someone, sometimes it's the subtle things that matter. Don't check your email, interact with your phone, or do anything else that shows they are not your only focus at the moment. If you don't show that they are worthy of your time, do you think you will be worthy of their time when you need their support?

>_ make people
   feel heard,
   valued, and
   appreciated

< 118 >

Give your dialog partner your full attention and allow them to be the center of your attention. When you do so, the engineers around will feel heard, valued, and appreciated. This also creates an environment that everyone wants to be part of.

Never Judge or Gossip

Never judge other people but rather shift your mindset so that you can learn something new from each and every person you interact with. Open yourself up to accepting a different viewpoint, to understanding someone else's belief system. Look upon others without condemnation. Remind yourself that you are not perfect and that too you have flaws of your own. Keep in mind that when you pass judgment on others, you define yourself as someone who feels the need to judge.

>_ gossip is the
   fastest way
   to erode
   trust

< 119 >

Similarly, never gossip or lie. Never, ever. Gossip and lies are the fastest way to erode trust. If you engage in gossip then people will instantly distrust you, because they will think you gossip about them behind their back as well.

Think about it: if you find out that someone speaks negatively about you, will you continue to trust or even support that person? Most certainly not. On the other end of the spectrum, however, if someone has your back and supports you even if you are not in the room, then you can be sure you have found yourself a friend and an ally for a lifetime.

Make It Easy to Correct a Problem

Giving honest, constructive, and sincere feedback brings people together, creates a healthy communication flow, and promotes personal and professional growth. It helps break bad habits, reinforces positive behavior, and enables teams to work more effectively toward their goals.

However, you will not accomplish anything by being overly critical or even harsh. You cannot change someone's behavior if you are offensive and demand that things need to happen differently next time around. The better approach is to be positive and focus on what can be changed and improved easily. One step at a time, little by little.

< 120 >

>_ accept apologies and focus on future improvements

Successful engineers are masters at giving positive feedback. Further, they are forgiving and can accept an apology if someone made a mistake. They instantly put their focus on what can be done better in the future. They foster team spirit by making it easy to correct a problem.

Saying Thank You Is a Powerful Tool

It's easy to pinpoint mistakes made by others. I have read countless emails where people complain about each other. However, pointing out the wrong behavior does not instantly cause that person to change. The better approach is to focus on good behaviors and what's going right. By encouraging someone to do more of the good things they are already doing, they will shift their focus and do even more of those good things. As a result, the compounding

< 121 >

effect of improvement kicks in. I have observed that successful people compliment, console, and congratulate to reinforce positive behavior. Let me ask you a question: have you ever written a thank-you note? Few people invest the time to send a thank-you note, but why? Think about it for a moment. If someone complains about you, what do you do the next time around? Most likely you will be even less likely to help that person, right?

>_ a thank you note reinforces positive behavior

In contrast, if you send a thank-you note and reinforce the positive behavior, you are more likely to steer the other person in the right direction. Even more powerful, write a thank-you note to the person's manager. It's a really powerful tool that builds positive spirit and fosters a can-do environment for everyone involved. Successful engineers know that a thank-you note goes a long way and can help you form allies for life.

< 122 >

successful
software
engineers

// nourish their
environment
because they
know they
cannot
succeed alone

< 124 >

CHAPTER 8

Ask Better Questions

»Successful people ask better questions, and as a result, they get better answers.« – Tony Robbins

Why is asking questions so important in software development?

Most fundamentally, it's a tool for opening up everyone on your team to exploring possibilities and creating solutions. Asking questions helps us clarify requirements, gather relevant information, and find creative solutions to difficult problems. It also provides a nourishing ground for clear communication, healthy interaction, and effective collaboration among team members.

In fact, I would argue that asking better questions is a uniquely powerful tool to advance your career.

However, there are big differences in the way individuals ask questions. Some people's questions help us see problems and evaluate solutions from a completely different angle. As a result, these people have a tremendously positive impact on how we collaborate. Other people's questions can steer a conversation away from what we are actually trying to accomplish - or, even worse, might generate a divisive atmosphere and thus have a negative impact on the entire team.

As you can easily imagine, people in the first category will achieve much greater success over the course of their careers than people in the second category!

>_ the way you phrase
   a question
   influences
   the outcome

< 126 >

By the end of this chapter, you'll have a clear understanding that how you ask a question significantly influences the answers you get and the outcome of asking. But let's start at the beginning and ease into this important matter by taking things step by step.

Start by Asking More Questions

First, it's always better to ask questions than to make assumptions, because assumptions set you up for failure. Assumptions cause you to misinterpret and misunderstand the situation you're in, whereas we want to set you up for success.

Generally there are many different circumstances where asking questions is beneficial. Obviously within an engineering team, you need to ask technical questions. But the spectrum includes requesting resources for a project and (everyone's favorite) asking for a raise or promotion. There's also the interpersonal aspect: you need to ask questions that show personal interest in other people. This kind of question helps to build trust and rapport with your peers, your team members, and your management chain.

Ultimately, the way you ask questions drastically shapes

< 127 >

your identity and how the people around you perceive you as an individual.

One of the basic benefits of asking questions is that it improves the exchange of information and fuels your learning. It allows for faster skill development, more exposure, new challenges, and therefore new opportunities for professional growth. In short, asking questions really helps to accelerate your career advancement.

>_ you participate
   differently
   in a conversation
   when you
   ask questions

Naturally, the initial step that most people take at this point is simply to ask more questions and participate more actively in conversations. One way to get started is by ask-

< 128 >

ing just one question in every meeting you attend. You'll quickly discover that you participate differently and listen more carefully when you hold yourself accountable to regularly ask meaningful questions. As a result, you'll find that information flows more freely and that you will start to absorb knowledge faster.

Ask the Right Question

Of course, simply asking more questions doesn't instantly improve the quality of a conversation or a team. For that, you need to ask the »right question«.

When you start to ask more questions, you become more attuned to how others ask questions and what answers they get. Soon you will realize that some engineers ask questions in a way that enables conversations to be more productive.

More specifically, the type, tone, sequence, and framing of a question can have a significant impact. Successful engineers know this and take advantage of it.

So, what does a good question look like?

First, it needs to be authentic, sincere, and honest. Don't ask a question if you merely want to make yourself feel important. Doing that accomplishes the complete opposite of what you want to achieve and causes people to become annoyed with you and even turn against you.

Second, it needs to explore the unknown. By that, I mean the answer shouldn't already be clear and given. Instead, a really vigorous question exposes what is not known. It should challenge you and your colleagues to admit uncertainty but also explore possibilities about the path forward.

Third, a powerful question is compelling and draws people into the conversation. Really influential questions even cause collective collaboration, generating energy and excitement to work together toward creative solutions.

Fourth, a really profound question is open-ended. The answer isn't a simple yes or no. To find the answer, everyone involved needs to think more carefully. In fact, that often leads to multiple answers and another round of questions, fueling even more creativity.

< 130 >

Fifth, a great question takes the long view and stands the test of time. It addresses a topic that matters not just for the next few days or weeks, but that will be relevant even five years from now.

Sixth and finally, the right question sets the stage for action. By challenging the why and the what, it focuses you and your team on what really matters to make a difference now and in the future.

For all these reasons, asking the right question is much more important than finding the right answer. That's because it gets everyone thinking and acting in truly creative ways and helps to foster a more creative environment in the long run.

>_ frame questions in an open-ended way

< 131 >

Question Yourself

During my years as a manager, I have realized that senior leaders are not only great at raising and formulating questions with others, but they also hold themselves to the same standards. They question everything they do and they get input and feedback from their peers to make sure they haven't overlooked anything of importance.

>_ challenge your assumptions and beliefs

For example, when senior engineers write a project plan, architecture document, or any other sort of strategy document, they ask people in their circle of trust to critique their work and what they have written before they publish it more widely. This helps them to challenge their own assumptions and beliefs. Quite often, beliefs that shape our understanding of a situation or topic are implicit. Sometimes, we hold onto certain beliefs or perspectives without

< 132 >

critically examining and questioning them.

However, questioning yourself and those implicit beliefs allows you to reassess and adjust your views as needed. Ask yourself: what evidence supports these assumptions? Are there facts, data, or experiences that validate them?

By questioning yourself and engaging with different sources of information and diverse opinions, you expose yourself to a variety of perspectives and challenge any biases in your assumptions. You also demonstrate that you have an open mind and that you are willing to adapt and change based on new information and experiences.

Further, questioning yourself and your work is a valuable and constructive practice for personal growth and self-awareness. Raising questions for your own work is also a critical part in any decision-making progress. It helps you to consider different perspectives, weigh pros and cons, and make more informed choices.

And, of course, it can save you from making serious mistakes or alienating potential supporters of your work!

Let me be clear: self-questioning doesn't imply self-doubt or criticism. It's about a constructive and inquisitive

< 133 >

exploration of your thoughts and behaviors to facilitate personal growth and well-being.

If You Don't Ask,
the Answer Is Always No

Before we close this chapter, I'd like to share a story that could change the way you think about questions.

One of my clients had been working in the same company for years and from what she told me did a great job in engineering. Her excellent work enabled her department to reach its goals for several years in a row. Her manager emphasized year after year that she is highly valued in the company. At the same time, she never really got a raise, let alone a promotion.

You already see where I am going with this story, right? She was always too scared to ask for a raise and hence her manager implicitly assumed that she was fine with the status quo. Because she never asked for a raise, she also never got one.

We worked together to help her build up the confidence to ask for a raise. First we created a list of all her accom-

< 134 >

plishments while with the company and in particular in the recent past. Next, we helped her craft a message that wasn't demanding or needy, but factual and confident. To do that, I encouraged her to think about what was important to the company and especially what was important to her boss.

>_ if you want something, dare to ask

We ended up doing some role plays and I gave her some tips and pointers. One of them was to wait for the right time. Most companies have some form of performance evaluation cycle and this is generally a good time to reflect on past accomplishments and to highlight successfully completed tasks and projects.

Ultimately my client was able to highlight her value and now had the confidence and courage to ask for a raise. In the short run, she got a significant salary increase and

< 135 >

a boost in self-confidence. In the long run, she learned a valuable lesson: »if you don't ask, then the answer is always no«.

< 136 >

successful
software
engineers

// ask the right
questions
and they know that
if you don't ask
the answer is
always
no

Beyond the Code

< 138 >

CHAPTER 9

Be Persistent

»We are what we repeatedly do.
Excellence, then, is not an act, but a habit.« – Will Durant

Persistence is absolutely one of the keys to success. Every great accomplishment takes years of preparation and practice. You must consistently practice the activity until it's so ingrained that it's like second nature to you. In short, you become what you repeatedly do.

Here's an example. Let's say you want to run a marathon. To finish the race, you'll have to run a little over 42 kilometers or 26 miles. If you think you can start preparing the day before, then good luck participating in the race. It

< 139 >

will be a very painful day for you. I can guarantee you that you'll never see the finish line. Most likely you won't even make it halfway through.

Anyone who wants to run a marathon needs to practice over a long period of time and build up to such a long race. What they do is build a habit of running several times a week, slowly increasing their distance so that when the day of the marathon comes they are ready to run the whole race.

It doesn't matter if the sun is shining or if it's pouring rain. They could stay inside instead of getting soaked, but they know they will not cross the finish line on the day of the marathon unless they are consistent and follow through on their training schedule. In fact, they don't focus on the rain but instead on their long-term objective: the major accomplishment of running a marathon. This is called delayed gratification.

The point is: if you consistently go for a run, then sooner or later you become a runner. Through all that running, you've been building and shaping a new identity. Slowly but steadily, you create an overlap between who you want

< 140 >

to be and who you are. This is the power of consistently, repeatedly working toward your goals.

>_ dedicate time to the skill you want to master every single day

This is true of any skill: you have to dedicate time every single day to practicing it, until it becomes second nature. Let's say you want to give a talk at a big technical conference. If you are serious about your goal, you start to practice, not only once, but consistently. You practice in front of the mirror. You record yourself and study the recordings.

You give a talk to your co-workers or a local computing club to gain more experience. You keep practicing, and you get a little better every single day. Put differently, you build public speaking in your daily routine. You start building a new habit and before you know it you will shape your new

< 141 >

identity as a public speaker. And by the way, nothing will change your life for the better than building new skills!

It doesn't matter what skill you want to acquire. You can learn any new skill, technical or not, if you want. The only ingredients you need are: consistency and discipline. Motivation will get you started, but discipline and consistency keep you going and growing.

Little Effort, Big Results

Have you ever wondered why some people are really good at something? Could be, they just build a habit into their daily routine and practice every single day. Like that runner out in the rain, people who become really good at something are committed to doing all the boring things consistently over a long period of time. Success is not a sprint, it's a marathon - not a one-time action, but a continuous process.

Here is a pragmatic suggestion on how you can boost your outcome without big effort. Start by dedicating a little bit of time during your day to become better at something. Don't overdo it, because very likely you'll throw in the towel and give up on it.

< 142 >

Start out with something you can do easily every single day. Let's go back to our example of running a marathon. If you make the commitment to run a marathon, then don't go out for a long run on the very first day. Chances are that your muscles will be so sore the next day that you will give up your ambition.

>_ build a daily
   routine around
   the person
   you want to become

Instead, go for a short run on the first day. You will feel a sense of accomplishment and you will feel that it was not so hard after all. The next day you will go out again for a short run. And so on. It might feel like you're only taking baby steps in the beginning, but you will quickly realize that »motivation comes from being in motion«.

Once you are in motion and you have done a multitude of short runs, you will feel like going for a longer run and

< 143 >

you will keep improving.

>_ doing small things consistently over a long period of time brings big results

Similarly, if you want to improve, or learn a new skill, then start small. Starting small, but doing your practice repeatedly, will lead to success. I cannot stress it enough: consistency is key. It's tremendously important to build a routine and follow through on it. A one-time action does not have any sustainability. Even more important, a lack of routine is a breeding ground for perpetual procrastination.

Here is a strategy that has proven successful time and time again. I know that a lot of successful software engineers have used this strategy to learn a new skill. Start out

< 144 >

by dedicating five minutes a day to practicing the skill you want to acquire or improve. Dedicating five minutes a day to something you want is so minimal, that you absolutely have no excuse not to do it. Right?

If you cannot find those five minutes, then you aren't really serious about your goals. Start small, but consistently do it, every day. You will find that small adjustments in your daily routine bring the results you want to show up in your life and career.

Start Today

Don't put off until tomorrow what you can do today. There is so much truth in that saying. In fact, it's more than a saying, it's an attitude and you can practice and learn to think that way. Recently someone told me in a 1:1 coaching session: »I set out to work on my master's thesis every day, but something more important always comes along and I can't finish it. I think I am going to drop out of school.«

Together we evaluated the situation. It boils down to this: Constantly procrastinating on a task will create such a massive mental mountain ahead of you, that eventually you will not be able to climb it.

< 145 >

Let's break that down further and evaluate what that means. I think we all agree that writing five sentences a day for a master's thesis is doable, right?

>_ postponing work
    creates a massive
    mental mountain that
    becomes hard
    to climb

If you don't write today, then you will need to write ten sentences tomorrow. If you postpone the work tomorrow, then you will need to write 15 sentences the day after tomorrow. If this spiral of constant procrastination continues, then the mountain of sentences you have to write will appear bigger and bigger. Eventually it will become a massive vertical face - so intimidating that you'll simply give up.

< 146 >

The best way to break that cycle right from the beginning is to make just a little bit of progress each day. Start easy and tell yourself, I'll just write two sentences today. Make it so small that you really have no excuse not to start working on it today. Again, you will see that motivation comes from being in motion. Once you start writing, you set yourself in motion and motivation kicks in.

By employing this easy mental trick, my client was able to finish her master's thesis. In fact she ended up writing more than the agreed-upon five sentences every day and it turned out to be an exceptional master's thesis.

Even though writing a master's thesis is a great example, the same reasoning holds true for so many other tasks that you keep postponing. Put in the work today, and remember: starting small enables you to finish big.

Being Efficient vs Being Effective

By now we have learned and internalized that being consistent is crucial. No doubt it is. However, there is a tiny trap that I want to help you avoid.

< 147 >

Being busy does not necessarily mean you are being productive. In fact, it could mean the opposite. One engineer told me that he is really effective at fixing problems in his application. He explained the software problems in detail and no doubt he was really efficient at fixing those bugs.

I love coding and in particular secure software architecture. Together we sat down and he guided me through the source code of his program. But he was so hung up on fixing those problems that at some point he forgot to take a step back and look at the bigger picture of the design of his software.

A not very complex re-architecture of the design within his core engine allowed him to eradicate an entire subclass of problems. Instead of becoming efficient at fixing individual problems, he managed to effectively eliminate the individual problems altogether.

As this example shows, consistently evaluating how you work is the path to success. Just because you have always done it that way, does not mean it's the most effective way to do it. Every now and then, take a step back and evaluate how you approach a problem.

< 148 >

Reflect on Yourself

Returning to what we have established earlier, consistency is key. That doesn't mean we should never modify or improve our processes. Every so often we need to update our mental operating system so we can keep performing at a high level. In other words, we need to reflect on ourselves.

Self-reflection is taking the time to think about how you tackle problems. It's about giving serious thought to your behaviors. To evaluate yourself, your attitude, your entire presence. If done at regular intervals, self-reflection in combination with intrinsically anchored consistency will set you up for success.

< 149 >

< 150 >

successful
software
engineers

// never give up
and know
that they become
what they
repeatedly do

BEYOND the code

< 152 >

CHAPTER 10

Don't Take Things Personally

»A man is not hurt so much by what happens, as by his opinion of what happens.« – Dale Carnegie

What does it mean to take things personally? In brief, it means you think everything is about you. You might even think you're so important that the world revolves around you. Of course it doesn't, but you might feel that it should. As a result, you will feel that your abilities, competencies, and achievements are constantly being judged and questioned by those around you. This can cause you to feel besieged and to dwell on what happens to you. It easily drags you down and consequently consumes a lot of your mental energy.

Quite often people take things personally when something »hits a nerve«. If you are not completely confident in your abilities as an engineer, or more broadly in your abilities in general, then you will be more inclined to project your own doubts onto other people. You will feel and perceive that people dislike certain aspects of yourself, when in fact you are the one who doesn't like those things.

As you can imagine, this way of thinking opens the door to a vicious cycle and has negative consequences for your emotions. It can lead to self-limiting beliefs and prevent you from pursuing your goals or reaching your full potential as an engineer.

>_ no one thinks
   as much
   about you
   as you do

< 154 >

Here's a story that illustrates the point. Two engineers were working on a big project together. Both were working on different tasks within different parts of the software stack, though still side by side. Both were technical experts in their field, both even had PhDs in Computer Science. They made architectural design decisions together, agreed on application interfaces, and shared status updates in the same engineering meeting each week.

As it happens, the economy went south and the project was canceled to save money. Both engineers were informed at the same meeting that they would be working on other projects starting the next day.

The first engineer was furious and yelled, »You can't do this to me, because I'm a great engineer and I've invested months of work in this project.« In fact, he thought he was sure to get a promotion and felt the company had taken that away from him. As you can see this engineer took it personally, reacted emotionally, and associated the failed project with his own failure - even though the cancellation was strictly a business decision.

< 155 >

By contrast, the second engineer demonstrated a high level of self-assurance and self-confidence. He remained calm and didn't get angry or lash out at his management. He was able to see things as they are and realized that the decision didn't have anything to do with the quality of his work. Instead of investing time and energy in resentment, he instantly put his gaze forward and focused on what was under his control - his new project and what he could learn and achieve there.

Which of the two do you think made the wiser decision? Which one is more likely to reach his full potential?

Successful engineers have internalized that the world does not revolve around them. They don't easily get offended and they work on constantly building up their skills so that they can remain confident in the face of adversity.

Don't Let It Get To You

Taking things personally leads to negative emotions and unnecessary stress. Here are a few suggestions for seeing things in a more positive light.

< 156 >

First, accept that someone's words and actions are often a reflection of their own beliefs, insecurities, and experiences, not a comment on your own worth. Understanding this helps you to maintain a broader perspective and to avoid internalizing everything as a personal attack.

>_ protect your
   emotional well-being
   and maintain
   a positive mindset

Second, by deciding how you will react to situations, you don't grant other people the power to hurt your feelings or make you angry. This way, you don't invest energy in things that bring you down, but instead transform that energy into personal growth, positive relations, and advancement toward your goals.

Third, assuming that someone's words or actions are intentionally directed at you can lead to unnecessary conflicts

< 157 >

because many disagreements are caused by simple misunderstandings. Allow space for open communication and give others the opportunity to clarify their intentions or provide context instead of jumping to conclusions.

Fourth, when you have a high level of self-assurance and self-confidence, your self-worth is not determined by the opinions or actions of others. This helps you maintain a strong sense of self and prevents external factors from affecting your self-esteem.

>_ direct your energy
   towards things
   that are
   under your control

In summary, consciously choosing not to take things personally leads to a more peaceful and fulfilling engineering life and directs your energy towards the things that make a difference in your career.

< 158 >

Comprehend Your Ego

The best way to learn to not take things personally is to comprehend your ego. In simple terms, your ego is your sense of self-esteem or self-importance.

Each and every one of us has an ego, which defines who we are or, more precisely, who we think we are. Although we create our own mental picture of ourselves, that picture does not necessarily map to the pictures that others have of us. These differences can have a major impact on how we connect and interact with each other, but to see how we first need to become aware of them.

>_ your
self-established
mental picture
of yourself
is different from
the one
others have of you

< 159 >

As one example, a person with a big ego can quickly generate emotions of discomfort, frustration, or even disdain within other people. No one likes to be spoken down to by someone who thinks they are superior, and they will often avoid working with such a person. That's not a recipe for career advancement!

The opposite of someone with a big ego is someone who is approachable, humble, modest, and down-to-earth. This kind of person encourages everyone around them to engage in the free flow of ideas, which is the essence of all learning, problem solving, and growth.

This is why I suggest you reflect on yourself and comprehend your ego. Instead of needing to be right, rather try to be kind. Your actions will speak louder than your words.

Remain Calm

No matter what happens and even in the midst of the wildest chaos, the most successful people manage to remain calm. The positive side effect is that calm is contagious, especially when the calm comes from the person in charge. If you lose your wits, if the group is completely

< 160 >

unsure of what to do next, it's the leader's job to remain calm, not by force but by example.

>_ remaining calm gives others the feeling that you have everything under control

Try to become the calm, relaxed person in every situation who tells everyone else not to worry, but rather to take a deep breath. Staying calm enables you to rise above the situation and to soothe everyone around you. Because this kind of feeling is contagious, you will be viewed as a person who has everything under control.

Here is my simple, pragmatic advice: Do not get upset. Getting upset about something colors the situation negatively and ultimately makes everything harder than

< 161 >

it needs to be. Remember the purpose and principles you value most. Running potential decisions through this filter will eliminate bad choices and enable you to stay on track even in difficult situations.

In summary, remain calm, do not get upset, do the right thing. It's quite simple, but admittedly easier said than done. Yet with practice you can make it happen.

Be Open to Feedback

Even though you shouldn't take things personally, you should still open yourself up to feedback. Ultimately all feedback, even if it seems negative at first, can be immensely positive. The reason is that feedback from your friends, peers, and managers will provide insights into your strengths and weaknesses. Hearing that feedback ultimately allows you to improve and advance your career faster.

Listening to and actively soliciting feedback fosters better collaboration among team members and promotes a culture of openness and collaboration, which is essential to the success of every software project and every software engineer.

< 162 >

Feedback from managers can also serve as an early warning system, allowing you to promptly detect potential issues and make the necessary adjustments. This openness to feedback and personal adaptability shows that you are mature and professional.

>_ start to view
   your peers as
   nice and decent
   human beings
   that want you
   to succeed

My attitude toward receiving feedback changed for the better when I started to view my colleagues as nice and decent human beings with good intentions who want me to succeed in my life and career. I figure that if they put in the effort to give me feedback, I should assume they do it to assist me in becoming more successful, not to hurt me.

< 163 >

Thus I try to absorb and incorporate whatever I can.

However, listening to feedback doesn't mean that I necessarily agree with it or that I change my behavior. It's healthy to recognize that feedback is sometimes nothing more than someone else's opinion. Consistent with the theme of this chapter, I don't let that kind of feedback get to me emotionally and I don't take it personally.

It's Nothing More than an Opinion

No matter what someone says to you, about you, or about the work you do, it's important to understand that their verbal statement is nothing more than an opinion.

Who says that this person is a source of truth? Maybe they are right, maybe they are wrong, maybe they have an agenda, maybe there is a kernel of truth in what they say. That's something for you to determine, not to blindly believe or feel bad about.

If you invest energy in feeling bad about what they said, then you are valuing their opinion more highly than your own judgment. Do not let external factors and other people's opinions affect your well being and your self-esteem.

< 164 >

>_ do not value someone else's opinion more highly than your own judgment

By acknowledging that it is just someone else's opinion, you minimize your own stress levels and open yourself up to a world of growth. And by not buying into that opinion and not getting offended, you come to better understand yourself and can invest your time and energy in things that move you forward. And what's more important than that?

< 165 >

< 166 >

successful
software
engineers

// never take
anything
personally
and focus on
what is
under their
control

Beyond the Code

< 168 >

CHAPTER 11

Make
No
Excuses

»The man who is good at making an excuse,
is seldom good at anything else.« – Benjamin Franklin

In the preceding chapters we have explored many characteristics and habits that successful engineers deploy to maximize their success and have an impact »beyond the code«.

In this chapter we will examine many of the excuses you could come up with, even the lies you could tell yourself, that could derail you from achieving your goals. We want to make sure that you don't subconsciously sabotage your own success without even realizing it. Rather we want you to be aware of your actions - and your lack of action - so you can take full control of where you are heading.

>_ excuses never lead the way to success

We will start gently by showcasing a few famous examples of excuses. Some might even sound familiar to you. Then we will move on to explore the nature of an excuse and ultimately we will discuss why we make excuses in the first place. We'll see that making excuses is just another way to avoid accountability. In short, excuses never lead the way to success.

Examples of Excuses

Here is a digestible but illustrative example that I have encountered multiple times in one form or another in my own career. As a software engineer and even more as an engineering manager, I have had the opportunity to screen

< 170 >

and interview countless candidates for open positions throughout the years. It was one of these days and someone was scheduled to come to our office in San Francisco to interview at 9:00am. The candidate kept me waiting for a while and I started to eagerly stare at my watch. Finally, I saw someone running down the street. The digital display on my watch showed 9:24 by the time he entered the office building.

When reaching to shake my hand he said furiously: »Sorry for being late, traffic was terrible this morning. And then I couldn't find parking, either.« While the stated facts were most likely correct, the underlying problem was not the traffic, and also not the admittedly difficult parking situation in downtown San Francisco.

No, the real problem was that the job candidate didn't add any buffer to his timing to account for commuting and parking. In the end, he used traffic and parking challenges as an excuse because he didn't want to be held accountable for being late.

Let's take this example one step further. Do you think it was important to the candidate to get the position? Did he signal that he would do almost anything to be part of that engineering team? Not to this interviewer! To me, the

< 171 >

signal was: »I don't care enough to show up on time.« And that translates to: »my time is more valuable than yours.«

In an earlier chapter we talked about how time is the most precious resource we have and we should be very careful how we make use of it. Letting someone wait, in particular when I want something from that person, definitely indicates that you don't have sufficient respect for the importance of that person's time. By contrast, successful people are always on time. In fact they always arrive early to account for any potential, uncontrollable, and unpredictable circumstances. And they value other people's time as much as they value their own - perhaps even more.

```
>_ if you do not
   make an effort,
   you value excuses
   over making progress
```

< 172 >

Let's look at another example. I was working with a client who wanted to take his career to the next level. Overall he impressed me as highly motivated. We were making good progress and eventually reached the point in our sessions where we were evaluating his communication skills and how he could improve. He said »I am horrible at public speaking.«

Before identifying precisely what we could do to improve his stage presence, I wanted to find out how serious he was about improving in this area. So I asked him to show me any recordings of himself speaking in public. He said he didn't have any because he never does any public speaking. I wanted to put him on the right track, so I followed up by asking: »How can you say you are bad at public speaking when in fact you are not doing it at all?«

Can you sense what I am trying to teach you? There is a big difference between being serious about eventually mastering public speaking (e.g., actively working to improve), and making the excuse that you are bad at it and hence not even trying.

No expert has ever fallen from the sky! Whatever skill you want to improve in your life, if you don't practice it, you

< 173 >

will never become better at it. If you don't make an effort, then you prefer making excuses over identifying opportunities and making progress. It's your decision.

>_ don't look for excuses but rather look for opportunities

There is a reason why successful engineers are so good at what they do. It's because they take their work seriously, they are honest with themselves, they take full responsibility for their progress, and they constantly practice the things they want to get better at. Instead of making excuses, they are always looking for opportunities to improve.

An Excuse Does Not Show the Way

An excuse is never the »real« reason that motivates our actions, or more accurately our lack of actions. No excuse

< 174 >

will ever change the situation for the better. If you want to become better at public speaking, give more talks. If you want to become better at writing proposals, write more proposals. Whatever it is, stop finding excuses for not doing it, and instead just do it.

Excuses are for people who refuse to accept accountability for their actions and their lack of action.

No matter how many excuses you can come up with, they will not advance your life, accelerate your growth, or set you up for success.

Once you realize that the excuses are not out there but in your head, things will change dramatically. Break free of excuses and be honest with yourself. I can guarantee it will change your life for the better.

Don't Confuse Excuses with Sunk Costs

Now that we have listed a few common excuses and we know what excuses are, we need to make sure we don't confuse excuses with sunk costs.

In business decision-making, sunk costs represent a cost that cannot be recovered and are contrasted with pro-

< 175 >

spective costs that can be avoided if appropriate action is taken. In plain English, a sunk cost is energy invested in the past. But the past is past and should never influence your decisions going forward. It's important to understand the difference, because sunk costs may act as distractors in decision-making and therefore might incorrectly provide fertile ground for yet another kind of excuse.

Let's say you invest six months in building a new feature for your application. After six months of hard work, you discover new market research data which reveals that no one even wants the feature.

The sunk cost fallacy might lead you to think: I already invested six months in programming that new feature, why should I throw it all away?

Understandably it's painful to admit that no one wants your wonderful new feature. However, the fact that you already invested six months in it should not influence your future decision making. In fact, that kind of thinking is just an excuse to keep working on the feature, perhaps because you've become attached to it or because you like how you architected the code. It's much better to simply move on

< 176 >

and avoid the prospective cost, which is far more expensive for your project and your career advancement.

Hold Yourself Accountable

By now we have established that an excuse is really just a misperception of reality. We use excuses to justify to ourselves why we did or did not do something. Unless you start holding yourself accountable for your actions, you will always find more excuses and you'll never make serious progress toward your goals.

>_ stop feeling
   like a victim
   and start acting
   like a winner

Instead of blaming things that are outside your control, ask yourself what you can change and what is under your control. Whenever something bad or unexpected happens,

< 177 >

ask yourself what you can control and how you can change the situation for the better, either right now or the next time around. Your mindset sets the tone for everything in your life. What you think and more importantly what you believe deep within yourself is what you act upon. Change your perspective going forward. I don't want to sound harsh, but stop feeling like a victim and start acting like a winner.

Successful engineers never feel like victims, they always take full responsibility for their actions. In fact, they also take full responsibility for their lack of action.

Sometimes they even take it one step further and hold themselves accountable for things that were never under their control in the first place. That's a truly impressive level of accountability!

< 178 >

successful
software
   engineers

// don't make
excuses but hold
themselves
accountable for
their actions
and also their
lack of action

< 180 >

CHAPTER 12

Commit
To
Yourself

»A winner is a dreamer who never gives up.«
– Nelson Mandela

Let me be clear right at the start: comfort is the enemy of success. As we've already discussed, you are the owner of your thoughts, feelings, and actions. This means you have a choice about the road ahead. On the one hand, you can live a life of comfortable mediocrity. On the other hand, you can commit to yourself and your aspirations, and thus make your dreams come true.

The choice is yours.

< 181 >

>_ you decide whether to live a life of comfortable mediocrity or to make your dreams come true

Successful engineers don't treat their aspirations as optional. Instead, they have an all-in mindset and a burning desire to succeed.

Successful engineers don't view their career goals as something that will just happen. Instead, they are well aware that winners put in the work and strive to get better every day.

In short, successful engineers know that they must »commit to themselves«. They might start small, but they constantly remind themselves that they can do it and over time they start to believe that they simply »will« succeed.

< 182 >

>_ constantly remind yourself that you can succeed

In their heart of hearts, they believe in the likelihood of success and they push beyond what other people imagine is possible. It's like the old story where everyone says a certain task is impossible. Then someone comes along who doesn't know it's impossible and simply does it.

The point is this: if you truly want to achieve something in your life, then you have to go for it. If you work on yourself and your mindset, if you push toward your goals as if your life depends on it, then you will put yourself on the road to success and I have no doubt you will succeed.

The Day Will Come

Here's a concept that my clients typically consider the most motivating of all when it comes to committing to yourself. Imagine you receive an email with the subject »Please celebrate with me in the auditorium this Friday

< 183 >

afternoon.« You kindly accept the invitation and show up in the auditorium on Friday. There are snacks, drinks, and some music in the background.

You chat with some of your colleagues and eventually someone walks up to the stage and speaks a few words. Suddenly you hear your name and you are asked to come on stage. Then it hits you: everyone in the auditorium is here because of you! It is your last day at work and you are attending your own retirement party.

Now, imagine you walk up on stage, take the microphone, and say a few words about your career. Basically you summarize all the highlights of your work life, your big accomplishments, your outstanding achievements, and the great people you worked with. What would you have to say?

Whenever I introduce my clients to this story and ask them to give a speech at their own retirement party, I can sense that they truly understand the big questions about their work: Am I committed to making progress toward my major goals? Does my current time and energy allocation align with what I want to achieve in my career?

From that point on, all the engineers that come to my highly individualized coaching sessions start to become really careful about how they invest their time.

< 184 >

>_ do not retire with your talent still in you

Truly successful engineers not only plan toward completion of their current project, but they plan years and decades ahead. In fact, they plan all the way to the end of their career and what they want to collect on their list of achievements. Do not retire without having accomplished the things you are meant to accomplish in your life and career.

You Have a Choice

Start by defining the North Star that will guide you all the way to your retirement party. As we have seen, you define your North Star by writing down your goals and by reviewing them on a daily basis. And remember, every day you have a choice and every day you can commit to moving one step closer to achieving your goals.

< 185 >

Do not unconsciously create tasks that keep you busy just for the sake of being busy. All that does is postpone your work on the most important tasks and projects, the ones you want to collect in your life resume. As a refresher, being busy does not mean you are being productive.

I cannot emphasize enough that it matters tremendously if you spend your time on low-value or no-value tasks, or on tasks that actually make a difference and contribute to your major goals.

Someone who took that concept to the extreme was Steve Jobs, pioneer of the personal computer era, co-founder of Apple and several other companies. Jobs was famous for always wearing blue jeans and a dark sweater. Have you ever wondered why? Because he didn't want to waste time figuring out what to wear for the day.

He was well aware that you can only accomplish so much in a day and he wanted to cut out all the meaningless tasks. By doing so, even in a small way, he kept moving closer to achieving his goals. And Steve Jobs certainly achieved amazing things in his life!

< 186 >

>_ you yourself decide how you invest your energy

Be honest with yourself and evaluate how you approach your day. Consistently ask yourself if you are really working on the most important tasks or not. You yourself decide. You must internalize that you have a choice and that you can make a conscious decision on how to invest your time and energy every single day. It's up to you whether you work on tasks that are meaningful and important, or tasks that distract you from the tasks that will advance your career.

You Deserve to Be Successful

Committing to becoming successful has numerous benefits and will positively impact various aspects of your life. Here are some compelling reasons why you should make that commitment to yourself.

< 187 >

First, achieving success can bring a deep sense of personal satisfaction and fulfillment. While success alone doesn't guarantee happiness, it enables you to recognize and utilize your potential, contributing to a more meaningful, purposeful, and satisfying life.

Second, success quite frankly comes with financial rewards. By committing to success, you increase the likelihood of financial stability, which will enhance your overall quality of life, for example by providing better healthcare, housing, and leisure activities. Additionally, it quite often opens doors to experiences and opportunities that may not be available otherwise.

Third, success enables you to have a positive impact on the lives of others. Being successful empowers you to support others and make a difference in your community or even the world.

Fourth, achieving success will drastically improve your self-confidence and self-esteem. The sense of accomplishment that comes with reaching your goals strengthens your belief in your abilities and motivates you to tackle new and exciting challenges as you grow older.

< 188 >

I can attest that all of the above statements hold true and that becoming more successful has had a tremendously positive impact on my life.

It's important to note that success is a personal and subjective concept. Your definition of success may differ from mine and from the definitions of others. The pragmatic advice I can give you is the following: align your goals with your values and priorities and do not compromise any of them.

Committing to success involves setting clear goals, staying focused, being resilient in the face of challenges, and continuously adapting and growing along the way. This requires a lot of hard work, but it is also tremendously rewarding.

Above all, remember: you deserve to be successful!

Sign a Contract With Yourself

Let me emphasize again that the key to becoming more successful is that you commit to doing so. Lots of engineers »want« to be more successful, but just »wanting« is

< 189 >

not enough. Wanting is just another word for hoping. Hoping that something will magically happen to make you more successful.

Do not wish for miracles. Do not hope that some outside force will come and save you. Luke and Yoda are busy doing other things. Only you have the power and ability to change your life for the better.

>_ you have all it takes to become highly successful

You have to let go of old routines and create new habits if you want to grow »beyond the code« and become truly successful. Remember, the way you think made you what you are today. Thinking the same way won't get you where you want to be. In fact, it does not get you where you deserve to be, because you owe it to yourself to be successful. And if you keep doing what you have been doing, then you

< 190 >

will keep getting what you always got.

Remember, thoughts lead to feelings, which lead to actions, which ultimately lead to results. You can choose who you want to become. You are the owner of your thoughts and actions, and you can decide to invest your time and energy wisely. Only in this way will you achieve the results you want to create in your life.

If you want to become truly successful, then follow the suggestions in this book, put in the work, and really commit to yourself. You can even think of it as signing a contract with yourself.

Yes, it's that serious!

< 191 >

< 192 >

successful
software
engineers

// commit to being
successful
and know that
they can become
who they
want to become

< 194 >

Summary
and
Outlook

»The future depends on what you do today.«
— Mahatma Gandhi

By now we have undertaken quite a journey together. To recap, technical skills are vital and it's important to keep improving your engineering capabilities so you remain at the forefront as a technical expert in the field. However, we have also learned that truly successful software engineers are not only technical experts but also adapt a specific mindset and apply certain habits so they can reach their full potential. We set out to transform your engineering life by evaluating the traits of successful engineers and by establishing a mindset of success within you, too.

< 195 >

Our overall objective was to align your actions with your goals. Hence we started by first determining your destination and figuring out what you really want to achieve in your life and career. And we reinforced the importance of believing in yourself and in your abilities to accomplish what you want.

Before closing I want to make sure you are truly set up for success and that you remember the core principles that will enable you to become highly successful as a software engineer. So let's quickly summarize and highlight the key takeaways from each chapter:

1. Write Down Your Goals: Identify what you actually want to achieve in your life and career and who you would like to become. Be honest with yourself, and really figure out what »YOU« want. Once you have identified what it is you actually want, it can become a tangible goal. Follow through and internalize your aspirations by making implicit information explicit and by writing down your goals. Writing down your goals enables you to create clarity for yourself and eliminate the surrounding noise of all the things that are not important. Get in motion, put in the work, and start to document your progress. Write updates

< 196 >

in your log book on a daily basis. Logging your progress helps stay you on track because it keeps your mind focused on the things that move you toward goals.

2. Make Every Minute Count: See every day as a new opportunity to make progress towards your major goals. Remember, you have a choice and you decide how to invest your time and energy. You can create tasks that keep you busy but don't move you forward, or you can make progress on the things that really matter. Make a conscious decision about how to invest your time. Make your time count. Remember what is under your control and what is not, what you can change and influence and what you cannot. Allow yourself to say 'no' - success does not come from taking on everything, but from focusing on a few things that really matter. Write scripts that assist and support you in your day-to-day activities. Doing so frees up your time so you squeeze value out of every minute and invest it in the important tasks that move you closer to your goals.

3. Cultivate Your Communication: The way you communicate has a massive impact on your career and success. Every signal that you send out to the people around you effectively tells a story of how good you want to be. Practice and cultivate your writing, speaking, and listening. Take the time to craft sophisticated, solid documents. Those artifacts will act as a business card for yourself and help others see how professional you are. Really start to listen to what people around you want you to know. Getting to know the people around you will build trust and rapport. You will hear when they struggle and need help, and you will learn what language sets them in motion. Take every opportunity to practice your public speaking skills, since this will bring people to your side so that they will assist you on your journey.

4. Create Solutions: Don't create problems, but create solutions. Don't focus on problems, but focus on opportunities. Carefully choose the problems you want to solve, because the problems you select define who you are and who you will become. Creating solutions takes time, but you will make steady progress if you focus on one bite at a time, continuously moving in the same direction. Get comfortable with taking calculated risks, because you cannot create solutions and become successful without taking risks.

< 198 >

5. Own Your Mistakes: Mistakes are not the opposite of success. In fact, mistakes build the foundation for all success. Do not perceive failure and mistakes as a negative, but rather as what they are: part of the process. Accept that you will make mistakes, maybe even a lot of them. Embrace your mistakes, do not blame others but claim ownership of your mistakes. Mistakes make you stronger and provide valuable opportunities for personal growth. Learn from them and use them to make better decisions in the future.

6. Seek a Mentor: A mentor is someone who is already years ahead on the path that you are traveling. A mentor assists you in setting goals but also ensures that you hold yourself accountable for achieving those goals. Having a mentor accelerates your professional development as well as your personal development. By establishing regular check-ins with your mentor, you will stay on track. A good mentor is by your side even when things get tough and ensures you never ever give up. Furthermore, being a mentor allows you to help others improve too and further strengthens your sense of purpose in life. So, not only have a mentor, but also be a mentor.

< 199 >

7. Nourish Your Environment: No matter how smart you are, you cannot do it alone. Support your colleagues, peers, and friends. If you nourish them and help them grow, they will help you grow in return. Keep in mind that success is not a zero-sum game. Instead, success compounds. Build allies and help your colleagues to improve, too. If you keep feeding and supporting the people around you, then they will support you and even want to see you win.

8. Ask Better Questions: Engage more in every conversation by asking questions, ideally by asking open-ended questions. Through asking questions you show that you are paying attention to the topic, that you care and are interested. Asking questions will force you to engage more in every conversation and enable you to gain more information more quickly. Remember, if you don't ask, whether it's to get more resources for a project or even request a raise or promotion, then the answer is always no.

9. Be Persistent: Don't wait for tomorrow, but rather put in the effort today. Instead of starting out too big and wanting to change everything all at once, it's better to make minor adjustments. Focus on the things you can do every single day to improve. The important thing is, do not

< 200 >

change course but stay on track, one step at a time. Many people overestimate what they can do within one month, but underestimate what they can do within one year if they consistently put in the effort. Put in a little bit of effort every day and you will see big results. Do not give up, ever.

10. Don't Take Things Personally: Never take things personally, it only leads to negative emotions and unnecessary stress. This protects your emotional well-being and allows you to maintain a positive mindset. You yourself can decide how you react to situations, and choosing not to take things personally will contribute to your overall success and happiness. Comprehend your ego and be humble and modest. Your actions speak louder than your words, anyway.

11. Make No Excuses: Hold yourself accountable for your actions and also your lack of action. Take complete ownership for your decisions. Do not look for excuses, but rather be honest with yourself and take responsibility. Stop looking for excuses and put in the work. Just do it.

12. Commit To Yourself: The key to becoming successful is that you »commit« to becoming successful. Remember, every day you have a choice and you can decide if you prefer to procrastinate or to put in the work and commit to yourself. Eventually the day will come when you retire. Make sure you have finished all the projects, have done all the things you want to claim at your retirement party. Create the results and the success you want to show up in your life.

Even though we are getting towards the end of the book, it is the beginning of your new engineering life. Before really closing I would like to give you one more thing to take with you on your path which is a key enabler for your success. It is tremendously important to acknowledge that we are all at a different point in our careers. We all have a different story, different background, history, gender, race, ethnicity, nationality, age and experience.

More broadly, we all grew up under different circumstances, in different parts of the world, enjoying different levels of support, or lack thereof. Some grew up with massive financial or emotional support from their parents, relatives, and friends, others with less and some with almost

< 202 >

no support at all. Put differently, some of us already had a rocky path behind us before we got to the point in our life where we were able to pick up this book.

All of us had to overcome different obstacles in our lives and sometimes it really seems that everyone else has it so much easier. However, please don't make the mistake of constantly comparing yourself with others. That is a race you cannot win and it will take energy and time away from the things that really matter on your journey to success.

Instead of comparing yourself with others, I suggest you rather compare yourself with your past self. In other words, focus on what is possible for you. After all, the only thing that really matters on your journey is the following question, which you should ask yourself every morning: Am I better than I was yesterday?

I encourage you to watch yourself, become conscious of your thoughts, your beliefs, your fears, your habits, your actions, and also your lack of action. Study yourself, or more elegantly, review the code you use to program yourself.

< 203 >

Finally, I want to close this book by saying »THANK YOU«. Thank you for your time and trust. I hope that everything turns out well for you and that in a few years you reflect back and think that picking up this book has had a positive impact on your career and ultimately on your entire life.

Go change the world and make it a better place. All the best, take care, and always remember:

You can do it!

< 204 >

A Tale of Extraordinary Willpower

»If you believe it will work out, you'll see opportunities.«
— Wayne Dyer

Lastly I want to share a story with you that keeps me going and motivates me personally every single day.

My early readers suggested that I cut it from the book because it has nothing to do with software engineering. They made a fair point, so initially I removed it. But eventually I decided to add it back, so I placed it here at the end of the book.

Here's why: at least for me and others I've shared it with, it serves as a great motivational tool.

< 205 >

I am sure you can find a similar story that matches your lifestyle and that you can identify with. Then you can bring that story to mind whenever you are in danger of falling back on old patterns or you need a boost in your willpower.

Probably this true story is so appealing to me because I love being in the mountains. In mountaineering, you constantly have to overcome obstacles to make it to the top. Sounds very similar to hiking the road to success, doesn't it?

This story is not about me, but about an individual whose name remains associated with extraordinary willpower like no other. His name: Hermann Buhl. Born in 1924 in Innsbruck, Austria as the youngest of four children, he spent years in an orphanage after the death of his mother. He, more than most other people, could have used the understandable excuse that his life was destined to failure because of this horrific loss so early in his life.

Perhaps, however, he somehow managed to turn that devastating stroke of fate into a sort of superpower. Perhaps he did not want to shatter from this painful experience, but rather shift his thoughts into a different, more positive direction. Perhaps he was able to trick his mind

< 206 >

and alter his beliefs along these lines: life has already given me a rough start, but in return what possibilities can it open me? Whatever the truth, it's hard to imagine a greater challenge than losing one's mother as a small child.

As a teenager, Buhl began to climb in the Austrian Alps, joining the Alpine Association and later the mountain rescue. He made his living as a guide and spent his days in the mountains. Being out on the rock almost every day, he soon mastered extremely difficult routes to the top. He was unreservedly committed to climbing and chalked up one summit victory after the other. His spectacular ascents and outstanding achievements quickly made him a well known and highly respected mountaineer. Not only in Austria, but also throughout the entire Alpine region.

In 1952 he was invited to join an expedition that would attempt to make the first ascent of Nanga Parbat. As I mentioned in the chapter »Seek a Mentor«, Nanga Parbat is an immense mountain in the Himalayas which is extremely difficult to climb and thus has earned the nickname »Killer Mountain« for its high number of climber fatalities. By the time of the expedition, 31 people had already died on the mountain and no one had made it to the top.

To conquer the mountain, one not only has to overcome the challenging terrain but also has to survive in the death zone. In mountaineering, the death zone refers to altitudes above 8,000m (26,000ft) where the pressure of oxygen is insufficient to sustain human life for an extended period of time. At that altitude, no human can acclimatize because the body uses up its store of oxygen faster than it can be replenished. An extended stay in the death zone without supplementary oxygen will result in deterioration of body functions, loss of consciousness and, ultimately, death.

July 1953, Buhl and his companions reached Camp V, the highest and last camp before the summit, at an altitude of 6,900m (22,600ft). They rested up, discussed their strategy, and decided how to proceed. The weather forecast was not promising and it seemed rather unlikely that a summit attempt could be started. For days the discussion among the expedition leaders had been around declaring defeat. Mood hit rock bottom amongst the mountaineers because their dream of reaching the top was about to come to an end. Exhausted from the climb and agonies so far, some of the other mountaineers decided to descend back to Camp IV at a lower altitude in preparation to leave the mountain and return home.

< 208 >

On July 3rd, 1953, at 2:30 in the morning, favored by a change in the weather, Buhl sensed a chance to attempt the summit. He decided to leave Camp V, alone and without additional oxygen. To paint a picture of the undertaking, Buhl was facing an arduous climb to the summit: 1,200m (4,000ft) of altitude difference and a distance of 6,500 meters (4 miles) through the death zone.

In your opinion, what were the chances that he would succeed and reach the summit? Bear in mind that the year was 1953. There was no high tech gear of the kind we have available today which would have assisted him in his undertaking. And don't forget, reaching the summit is only half the battle. He had to master the descent back to Camp V, too. And again, he was all by himself. No one to take turns blazing the trail and no one to encourage him.

If you were to ask me about the probability that he could reach the summit, alone, in deep snow, gusty winds, and freezing temperatures - I would say his chances were very close to zero. What about you? How would you rate his chances?

< 209 >

Ultimately, however, it does not matter what you believe, what I believe, or what anyone else believes. Because, above all else, Buhl believed in himself. He believed in his abilities and he believed it was possible for him to conquer the mountain. He believed he would succeed and be the first human being to reach the top of Nanga Parbat.

And he did. At around 7pm and with the last of his strength he reached the summit an astonishing 17 hours after he started out at Camp V. That by itself already demonstrates his dedication and his will to succeed. He celebrated his victory for a few moments and rammed his ice pick into the snow. He left it there as a proof that he actually made it to the summit. He really did it! What an extraordinary achievement! Unbelievable, in my opinion.

As soon as the initial excitement from his heroic triumph had passed, he realized that night was falling and he needed to start his descent. Instantly, it became obvious that he could not make it all the way down to Camp V in time. It was getting dark, and he was exhausted and drained from the hardships so far. The possibility of slipping and falling to his death became too big of a risk for him. He knew he had to spend the night on the mountain.

< 210 >

Not only that, he also knew he had to spend the night in the death zone.

Giving up had never been an option for Buhl. Yet again he managed to remain positive. He believed in himself, and he endured a bivouac at 8,000m (26,200ft). A bivouac is nothing else than a temporary camp, though without any cover or tent. In fact, he did not have any kind of protective equipment at all. He spent the night standing untethered on a tiny outcropping of rock too small to squat upon. There were no ropes to save him from a drop into the sheer abyss underneath him in case he fell asleep.

Let's come back to the question we raised earlier. How would you rate his chances for survival at this point? Almost zero, or zero point zero? But hey, we are talking about Hermann Buhl here! Through force of will he stayed positive. He believed and he encouraged himself to stay awake. Here again, he believed in himself and that believed it was possible for him to make it through the night.

And again, he did it. He returned back down to Camp V under his own power, mastering the strenuous climb to the summit and subsequent descent in an almost unimaginable

< 211 >

41 hours. Unbelievable. Outstanding. Simply heroic in my opinion. Buhl's solo ascent of Nanga Parbat is certainly one of the most amazing feats in all of mountaineering. Not only because it testifies to years of preparation and unbelievable physical performance, but above all because it demonstrates the mental strength of an extraordinary person.

He is often quoted as saying: »Hours before I reached the summit I thought to myself: I am so exhausted, I can't climb any further.« By which he meant that he was physically so exhausted from the climb that he could barely put one foot in front of the other. And still, his intrinsic motivation kept him going. He constantly reminded himself that he would succeed by saying to himself »I can and I will.«

The fact that Buhl believed in the feasibility and success of his summit ascent makes it clear that he was able to push beyond what others imagined possible.

Now, I certainly understand that what Buhl achieved is outstanding and even borderline crazy. Some might even argue: What's the point? If he had failed, he would have

< 212 >

died. No success, no trophy, no reward can be big enough that it is worth dying for. Fair point. However, because he believed in himself, he was able to achieve something that no one had ever done before. You have to admit that his self-confidence, his certainty that he would reach the summit, was truly remarkable.

Hermann Buhl knew that if he stood still, that if he stopped moving, even for one minute, then his dream, his vision, and his ultimate goal would die along with him on the mountain.

What can we take away from his achievement? If you truly want to achieve something in your life, then you can create for yourself a kind of life-or-death-mentality about how important that achievement is.

I understand that you and I are only software engineers, not mountaineers. But the underlying concept and reason for success is the same: the can-do attitude which Buhl personified to the nth degree. If you are really serious about your aspirations, as no doubt Buhl was serious about his, you can create an all-in mindset that enables you to overcome all the obstacles that would otherwise block you on

< 213 >

your path to success. Similar to Buhl, you can constantly say to yourself »I can and I will.« With this simple mind trick, you will remain decisive and on track. You will push through difficult times and keep yourself motivated. You will keep going even if you feel tired and exhausted. Even better, the more often you say it to yourself, the more you are going to trust it. You will start to believe in yourself and your abilities, and your self-esteem will grow with it.

When I feel tired, I try to picture how tired Buhl must have felt. When I am exhausted, I try to imagine how exhausted Buhl must have been. If Buhl could do it, then I can do it. And if I can do it, you can, too. You can follow Buhl's example and create for yourself the life-or-death mentality that he embodied. You can create such massive strength within yourself that you will push through any potential blocker, because you know that your life depends on it.

You can do it!

< 214 >

< 215 >

< 216 >

Thank you
to my loving and supportive wife, Sabine, and
my dear children, Nora, Ben and Lara.
What would success even mean without you?

< 217 >

< 218 >

Thank you
to all the fabulous human beings,
the engineers that I have met along the way
in my over 20 years in the industry, and who
taught me so much about how to succeed, so
that I can pass those lessons
on to you in this book.

< 219 >

< 220 >

Finally I wish to extend my profound gratitude
to Peter Saint-Andre,
an outstanding human being, friend, mentor,
and editor of this book.
Thank you!

< 221 >

< 222 >

About the Author

//

Dr. Christoph Kerschbaumer has over two decades of experience in software engineering and computer security. His work ranges from designing secure systems with fail-safe defaults to fighting cross-site scripting to preventing man-in-the-middle attacks.

He received his PhD in Computer Science from the University of California, Irvine, where his research focused on information flow tracking techniques within web browsers.

Prior to being a graduate research scholar, he received a M.Sc. and B.Sc. in Computer Science from the Technical University Graz, Austria.

//

For more information, please visit:

https://christophkerschbaumer.com

< 224 >

www.ingramcontent.com/pod-product-compliance
Lightning Source LLC
Chambersburg PA
CBHW050440290526
45786CB00006B/2095